Picture Yourself Fishing!

Picture Yourself Fishing!

Pacific Northwest Pictorial & Fishing Journal.

By: Elizabeth Rhodes Moffett Musician, Artist, Writer, Photographer & Fisherman.

Published by Tablo

Published in 2020 by Tablo Publishing.

Publisher and wholesale enquiries: orders@tablo.io

20 21 22 23 LSC 10 9 8 7 6 5 4 3 2 1

Table of Contents

Lewis River

Like almost all Native tribes, Indigenous groups on the Lewis River experienced a population collapse as a result of an 1830 epidemic introduced by early colonizers. This is one of the reasons many early recorded observations include large shifts and changes in tribal populations. Tribal listings compiled by anthropologist Verne F. Ray mention a village about 5 miles (8.0 km) upstream from the mouth of the Lewis, which was originally populated by the Cowlitz, but transitioned after 1830 to a Klickitat population. Lewis and Clark encountered a tribe on the Lewis River that they referred to as "Cathlapotles," which are thought to be Chinook, but they also recorded a Sahaptin-speaking village near the mouth of the Lewis, which were likely Klickitat people.

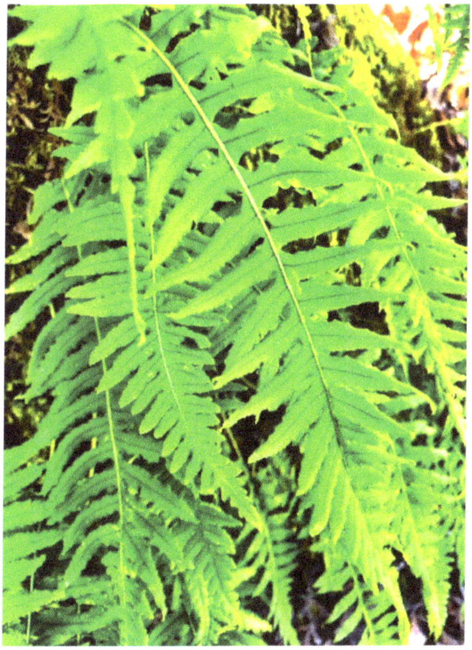

"I was raised in a family of colorful story tellers. If you were too, we could be here all night. See beauty everywhere. Read the skies, listen to the earth and feed your soul." Local Photographer: Elizabeth Rhodes Moffett

On of the first recorded sightings (by a non Indigenous person) of the Lewis was in 1792, when William Robert Broughton passed the mouth of the Lewis while exploring the Columbia River during the Vancouver Expedition. He named it Rushleigh's River at that time. At the time Lewis and Clark crossed the river, they had already named the Snake River the Lewis, and referred to the present-day Lewis as the Cathlapoote. Other historically recorded names include the Kattlepoutal and Washington River.

The Donation Land Claim Act of 1850 brought an influx of colonizers to the region, but just prior to that in 1845, Adolphus Lee Lewis retired from the Hudson's Bay Company and established a land claim near present day Woodland. Lewis became the county surveyor in 1856, and applied his own name to the river. Source: Wikipedia

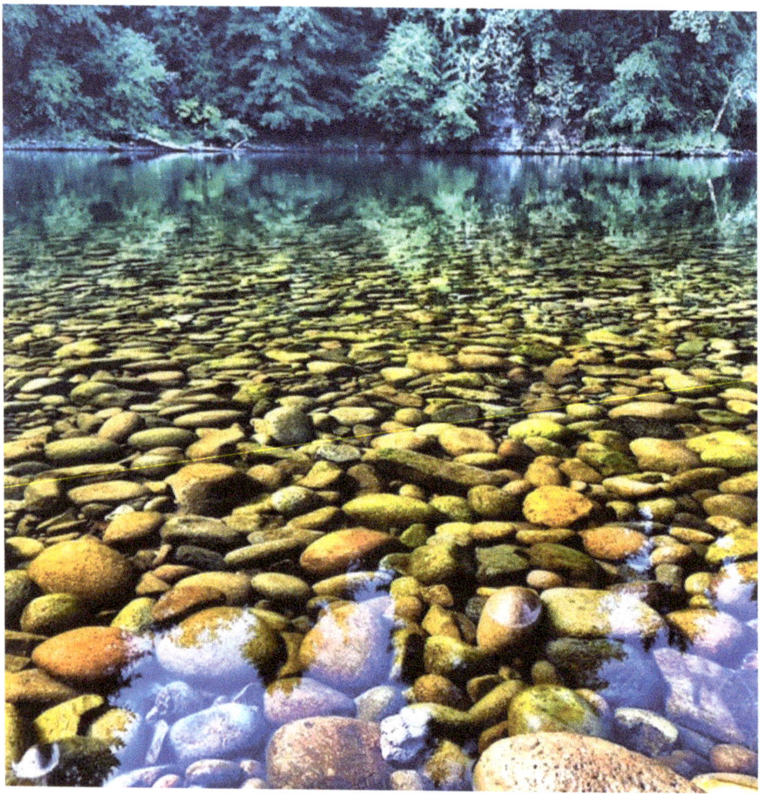

The Lewis River is magnetic. Incredible rock hunting. Agates, volcanic rocks and healing crystals can be found here. Magical at times, I lived on the Lewis River for five years. “Nature can heal your spirit, I am here to tell you the truth.”

Lewis River Fishing

By Carter Reschke   BestFishinginAmerica.com

Situated just north of the Oregon-Washington border, the Lewis River is one of the Columbia River's most popular and productive tributaries.

The Lewis River is a long one, and it is dammed three times, creating three formidable reservoirs: Lake Merwin, Yale Lake and Swift Reservoir.

These reservoirs are essentially back-to-back, and there's not much river in between. For the purposes of this article, we'll be referring to the lower river (below Lake Merwin) and the upper river (above Swift Reservoir).

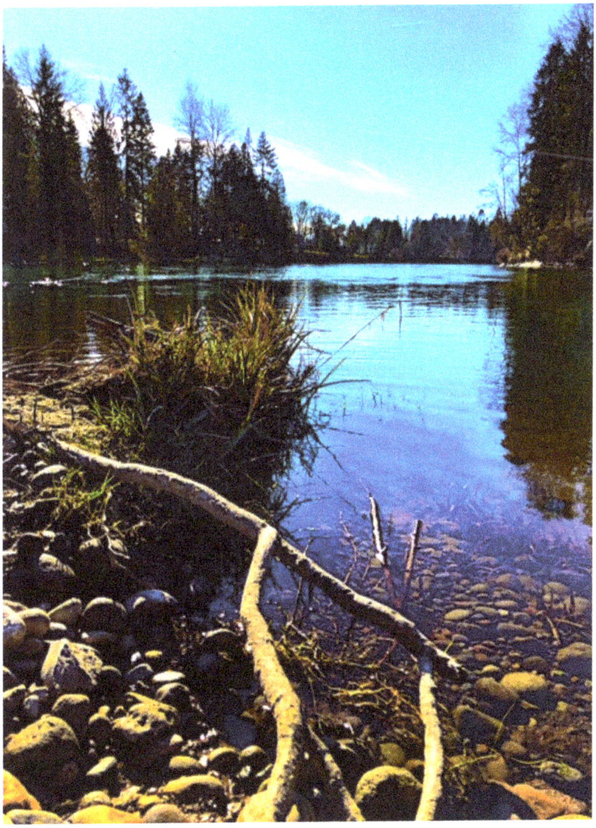

A local hang out for great fishing and lively conversation. While I lived there, we called it, the point. My Friends knew if I didn't answer the door, I was at the point.

The mainstem Lewis, often called the North Fork Lewis, is popular with steelhead, salmon and trout fisherman alike. It's also a pretty good fly fishing river.

Anglers, especially steelheaders, also commonly fish the East Fork in Clark County, which we'll tackle after discussing the larger river.

Each stretch of the river offers different opportunities, and diverse riffles and runs lurk around every corner. If you're looking for some reliable fishing action, the Lewis River is a great spot to go.

Let's dive into the primary differences between the upper and the lower Lewis.

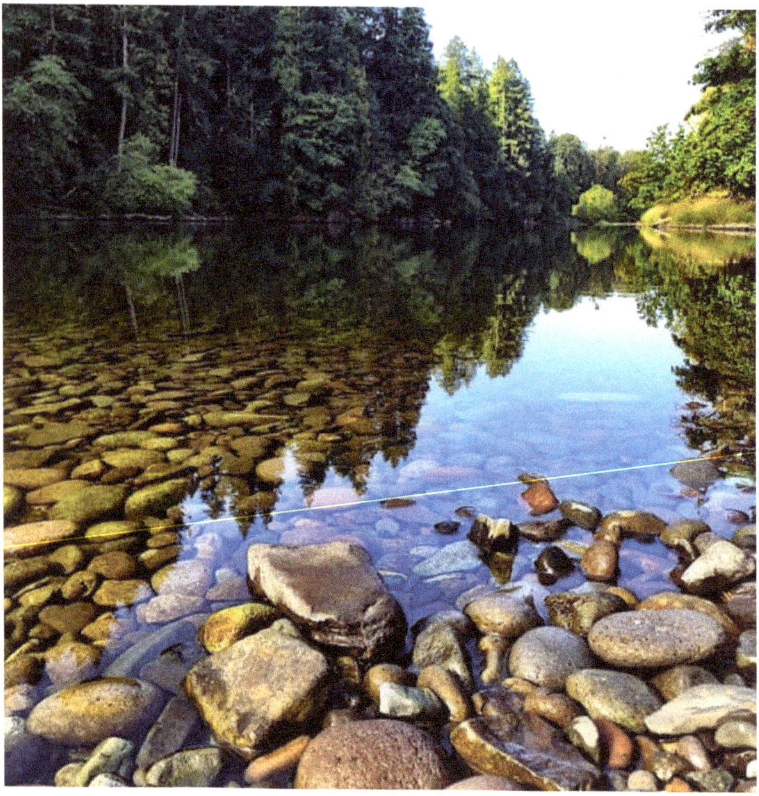

The Lewis taught me about photography, healing and fishing. Would walk here daily and and often would visit at night.. The Moon and stars are so bright here. It changes you Inside.

Fishing on the Lower Lewis River

By far the most popular stretch of the river, the lower Lewis River is home to often-plentiful runs of salmon and steelhead.

This is where you'll see most of the angling pressure – the lower Lewis runs from Lake Merwin down to the mouth of the river near Woodland, a section of water stretching approximately 20 miles.

We'll talk more about how to target the salmon and steelhead in the Lewis later on in the article, but know that if you're thinking about salmon fishing, the lower Lewis is the place to be when runs are good.

This is a stretch of water that's best fished by boat. Whether you've got your own or you book a guide, you'll be a lot more successful on the lower river if you have a drift boat or raft so you can access the prime water.

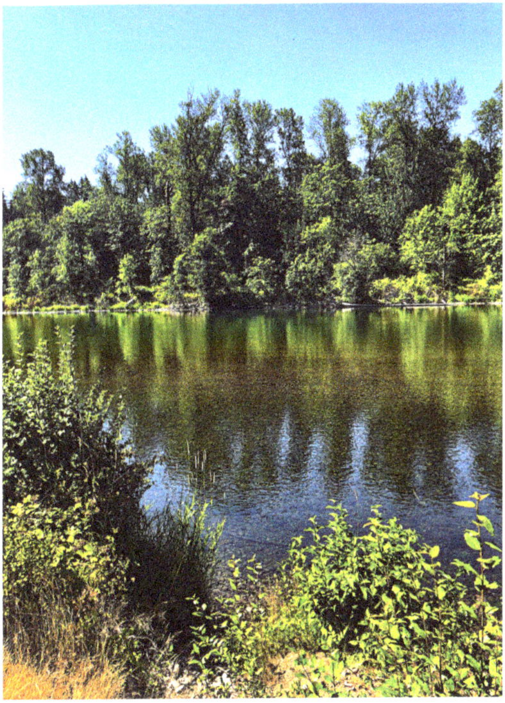

Fun Facts: My Grandpa Lewis worked at the Lewis River Fish Hatchery on the Lewis River. No relation to Lewis & Clark, however it was fun to name drop at local pubs.

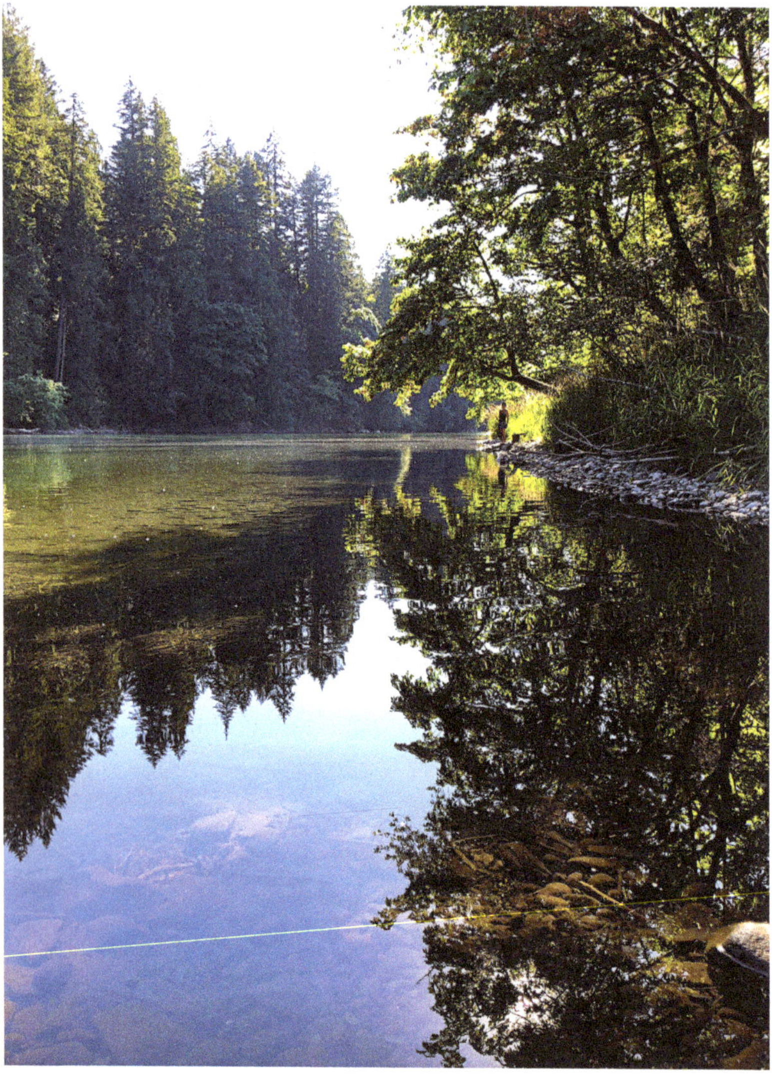

Not often you have a glass river. Sometimes, like us, they settle and seem to rest. Long summer days, we would walk to this spot. The light was perfect. We stayed a long time that afternoon finding agates and feeling the peace.

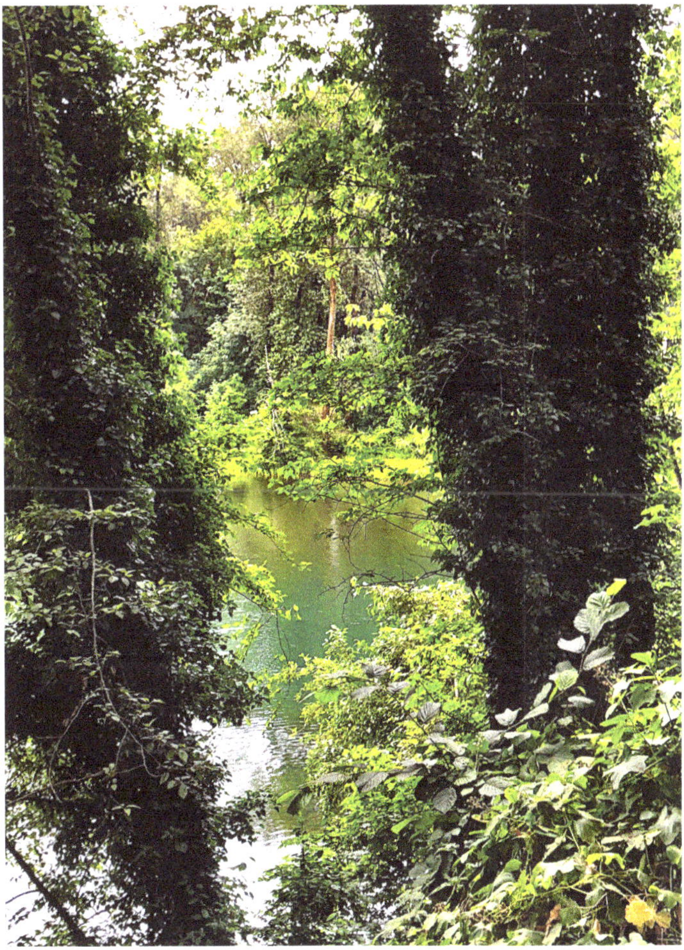

I spent time experimenting with photography. Every day is a different color.

Fishing on the Upper Lewis River

The upper Lewis is somewhat of an undiscovered gem. You may see another angler or two out on the water, but for the most part, it gets overlooked for the much more popular lower stretch.

However, the upper Lewis River is a great spot for fly fishermen in search of some classic, small-ish stream trout fishing.

Rainbow, cutthroat and bull trout all inhabit this portion of the river, but you may not target the protected bull trout and must release them unharmed if you catch them. Bull trout can grow to impressive sizes in the Northwest but their populations have suffered in many areas.

Fishing is catch-and-release for all wild rainbows and cutthroat as well, but there is a very short section of river (a mile or less) right above Swift and below the junction of Muddy River where you may retain hatchery rainbows, identified by a clipped and healed adipose fin.

These hatchery trout aren't stocked in the river but are planted in Swift and may venture a short distance upstream.

As you head upstream, the Lewis gets smaller and smaller (and so do the fish).

It's a fun experience for an adventurous fly fisherman, and while the upper Lewis isn't nearly as popular as the lower stretches of the river, it's still a great spot to check out.

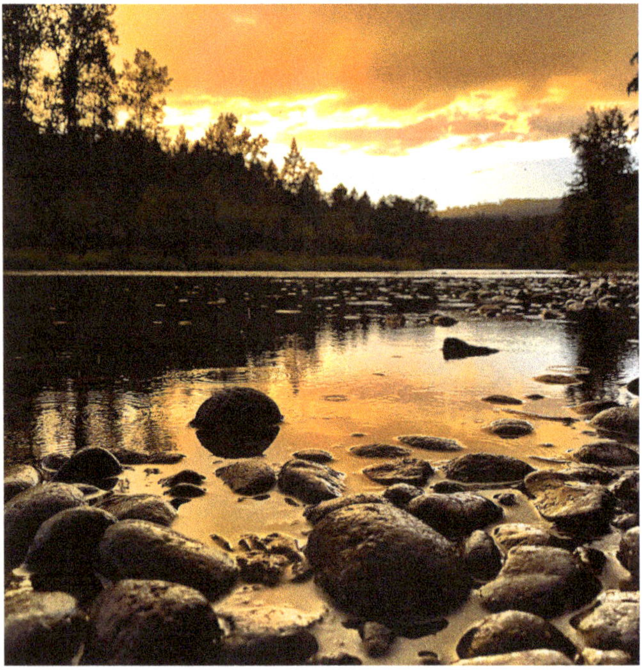

Faithful rainstorms contribute yearly to her natural beauty. The birds became quiet. Rain drops fell and she cried with me that night. Listen to the animals, they are trying to teach us.

Salmon Fishing on the Lewis River

As we mentioned above, all of the salmon fishing action takes place on the lower 20 miles of the Lewis, where these migrating fish have access to the Columbia River down to the Pacific Ocean.

Chinook salmon make their way into the river in both the spring and the fall, while the coho run (like all other rivers in the PNW) occurs during the fall.

June is usually a peak for the spring Chinook run, while September and October are typically the most reliable for fall Chinook and coho.

Always check the latest regulations, though, because WDFW will close down salmon fishing the Lewis (as in other waters) if the returns are expected to be poor. But when runs are good, this is can be an excellent destination.

Both types of salmon are fun to catch, and the coho in the Lewis are known to grow quite large.

Catching these salmon is quite typical to most other rivers in the region.

The Lewis is best fished by boat, and bobber-and-roe tactics typically are king when it comes to fishing for Chinook, which often respond to bait.

Coho can be more aggressive at times than Chinook, particularly when they are freshly arrived in the river, and it's a good idea to try swinging a few spoons or spinners through some of the swifter water.

As a general rule, coho hang out in water that's faster and shallower than what Chinook prefer – this isn't always true, but it's a good rule of thumb to go by as you're fishing the river.

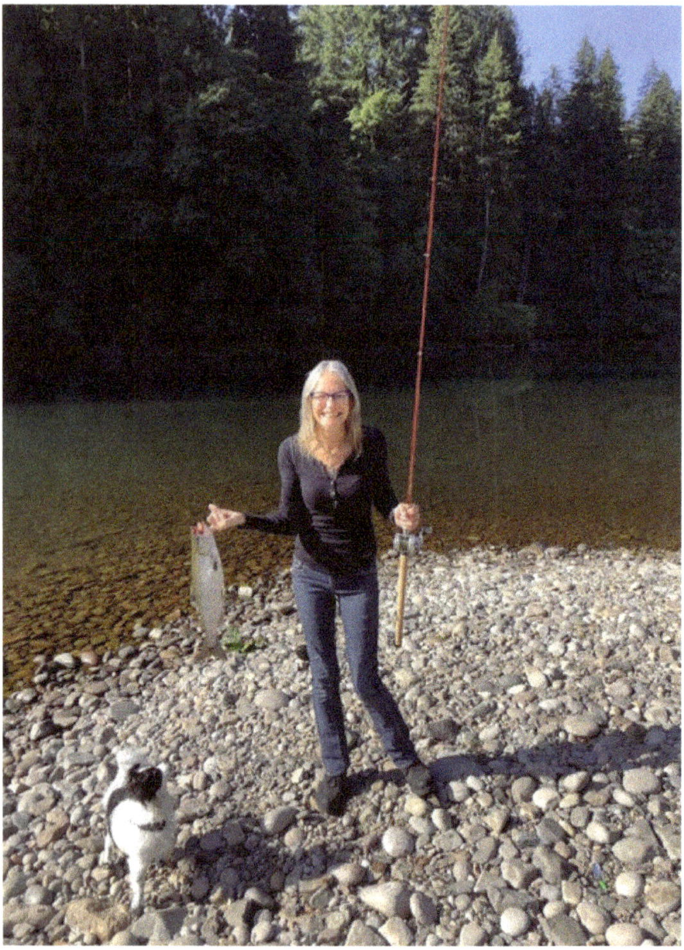

Buddy Love fishing the Lewis River, Woodland Washington. It was our first date!

Steelhead Fishing on the Lewis River

Unlike salmon, steelhead hang around in rivers for a while after they spawn, and some steelhead end up returning back to the ocean. Due to this behavior, you can find steelhead in the Lewis River year-round.

The Lewis receives both summer and winter runs of steelhead.

The summer fish show up starting in May and June, with the run peaking sometime during July or August.

The winter fish, which are often bigger than the summer fish, show up in good numbers during December, with best fishing in December and January. Some winter fish hang around into late spring or early summer but their quality diminishes over time.

A bobber and jig is a great way to catch steelhead on the Lewis.

If a jig isn't working out for you, try tipping the jig with a prawn – that can sometimes be the difference between getting skunked and catching a steelhead or two!

Both the steelhead and salmon seasons can change year-to-year, so be sure to keep up with the current regulations. The river is open nearly year-round, but not quite – so check before you get out fishing.

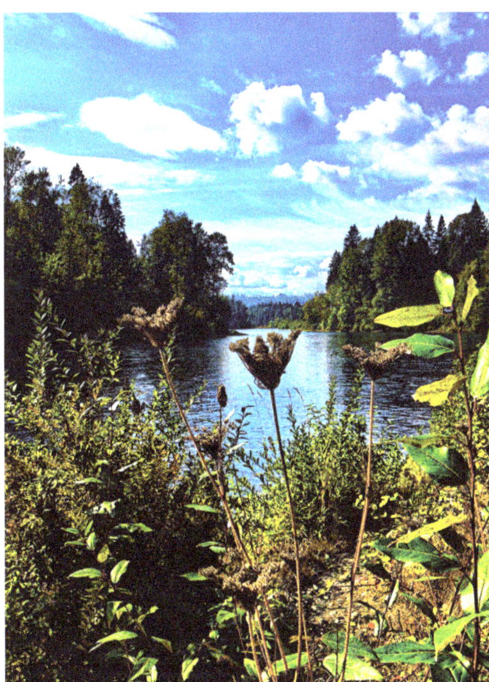

Cowlitz County hides a wealth of culinary harvest. Pacific Northwest Salmon, Grapes, Blackberries and Mushrooms are in high seasonal demand.

Trout Fishing on the Lewis River

Bull trout, rainbow trout, whitefish, and cutthroat trout are all officially in the Lewis River. The most common catch will be rainbow and cutthroat trout, though you'll see a bull trout or whitefish in the mix occasionally.

The majority of the trout fishing on the Lewis River is done above Swift Reservoir, and it's most popular with fly fishermen and is primarily catch-and-release except in that area right above the reservoir where there might be a hatchery fish.

Conventional techniques such as spinners (and other artificial lures) are allowed and will catch fish as well.

If you're fly fishing, try standard attractor nymphs.

There's nothing particularly special about the bug life on the upper Lewis, and you won't see a ton of prolific hatches.

Pheasant tails and hare's ears are great patterns to try out.

If you're euro nymphing, the standard patterns will work wonders: think perdigons, frenchies, and the like.

There isn't a ton of dry fly activity to be had on the Lewis River, but if you're itching for some dry fly eats, a size 14 stimulator is a good bet.

You might not catch the biggest fish, but there are eager rainbows and cutthroat in the river that aren't very picky.

And, again, remember you can't legally target the bull trout here and you must release them unharmed if you do catch bulls.

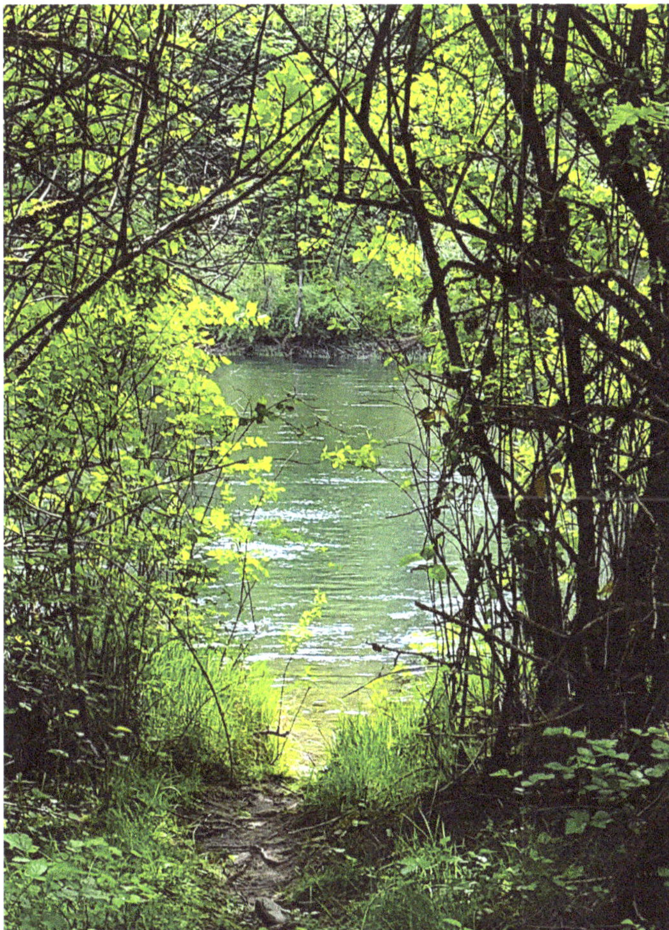

The Lewis is a tidal river. Like life, it has highs and lows.

When to fish the Lewis River

The Lewis River offers spectacular fishing opportunities year-round. If you're trying to figure out when to get out there, first decide what you want to fish for.

Want to try for some steelhead? Summer and late winter are great times to fish.

Salmon? Try spring and fall.

Or, if trout are what you're interested in, the late spring and early fall are great times to fish.

Fortunately, winters don't get brutal on the Lewis – because of its location, you'll typically see mild winter weather, with temperatures in the 40s and rain being much more common than clear skies.

If you're planning to head out to the Lewis in the winter, be sure to check river conditions before you do – the heavy rainfall can make the river high and unfishable quite frequently during the winter months.

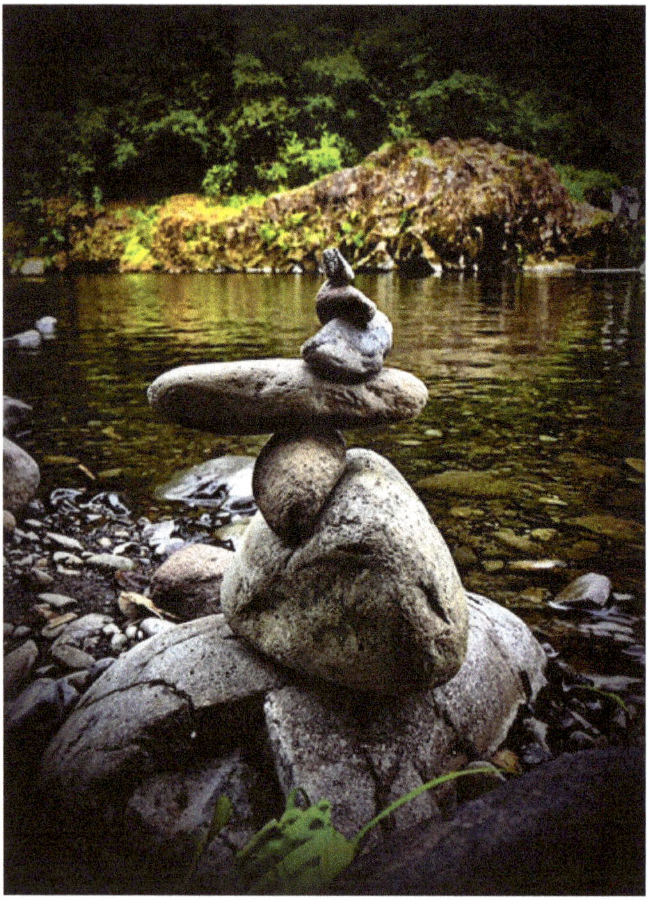

I possess this strange talent. If you look closely, this should not work. I have studied this more than I would care to reveal. Very proficient in balance. I do not know why I do this.

Location and Access

The lower Lewis River is in a convenient location if you're living near Portland or Vancouver. It's just off of I-5 near Woodland, and makes for a great day trip if you're not looking to drive very far.

The upper Lewis, however, is a slightly longer drive.

Once you get off I-5, you'll make your way east on State Route 503 (and then Forest Road 90 farther upriver) until you get above Swift Reservoir, which can take a couple of hours if you're coming from the Portland area.

There are numerous boat ramps on the lower Lewis River, and access isn't much of a problem if you've got some sort of suitable watercraft like a drift boat.

On the upper river, though, you'll be bank fishing. There are a few access points at bridges, and since the river is easily wadeable, you'll be able to walk up and down to explore new water.

A couple of lightly used trails (likely made by anglers) run along the upper river as well, making it fairly easy to navigate. It's not the spot to go if you don't like a bit of hiking, but if you're one for exploring, the upper Lewis is great.

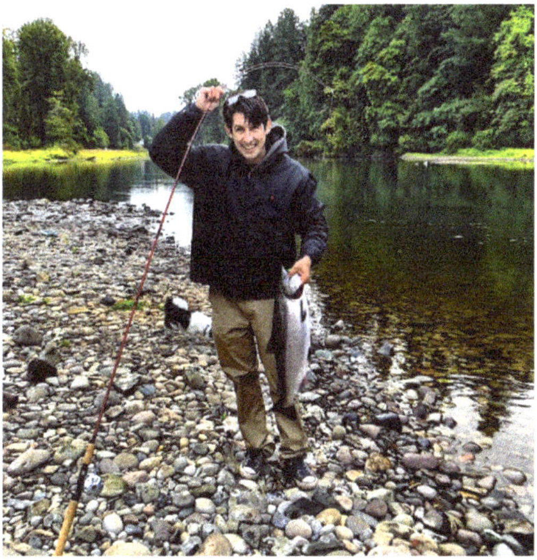

Darold and Buddy Love with an early catch in his work pants.
What a fantastic morning. We were all hooked.

Fishing the East Fork Lewis River

The east fork is the smaller of the two forks.

It headwaters in the Gifford Pinchot National Forest and generally flows south of the main Lewis, which it joins in the lower reaches near Interstate 5 after passing through Clark County.

Among anglers, the East Fork has been most famous for its steelhead runs, which years ago produced not only high numbers but some mammoth specimens. A state record winter steelhead caught here in the 1980s was nearly 33 pounds.

Unfortunately, the East Fork isn't nearly the steelhead river it once was, although it still puts out both summer and winter fish produced in hatchery programs.

Runs throughout the region are cyclical, so an upswing of Northwest steelhead in general should mean better angling here as well.

There are river access points including Lewisville and Daybreak regional parks in the Battle Ground area, and you also can float from launches at Lewisville to Daybreak with a drift boat.

There are some additional boat access points farther downriver as well, but Lucia Falls and other drops are located upstream.

Trout and salmon fishing are highly regulated on the East Fork Lewis to protect sensitive fish species, so definitely give the regulations a careful reading and probably head to the North Lewis or other locations to catch those fish. Source:

The Lewis River is a great option for some Washington fishing that's not too far from Portland and Vancouver!

If you're looking for some productive year-round fishing, this is a great river to check out. Tight lines.

Thank you BestFishinginAmerica.com Article By: Carter Reschke

Special Thanks to Eric Apalategui for permission on Carter's Fantastic Article. "I couldn't have said it better myself." Elizabeth, UpriverStudios

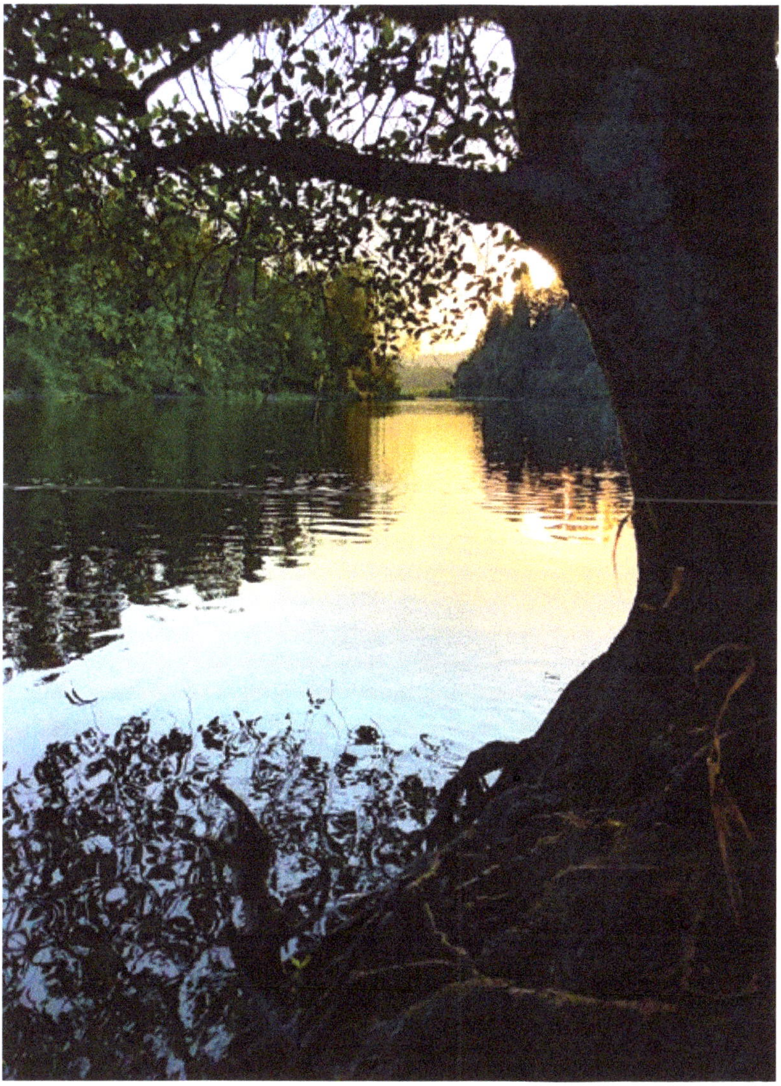

I adore hot summer nights in nature. I watched the sun set and stayed until I could see the stars. Walking home across the dark Golf Course, the full moon was brilliant. I love looking at the stars. When I left home as a teenager, I assigned family members to constellations in the night sky so I can always visit them. Mother is Cassiopia. Brother Dan is Orion. Dad and I would look for the Big Dipper together and I am the North Star.

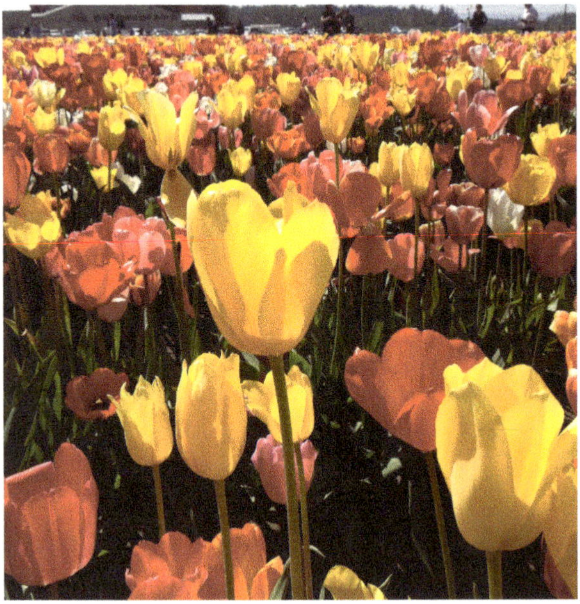

Tip for photographers: Nearby is the World Famous Holland Bulb Farms. Great time for a spring photo shoot. It is a visual explosion of color. I visit every spring. So fun and inspiring.

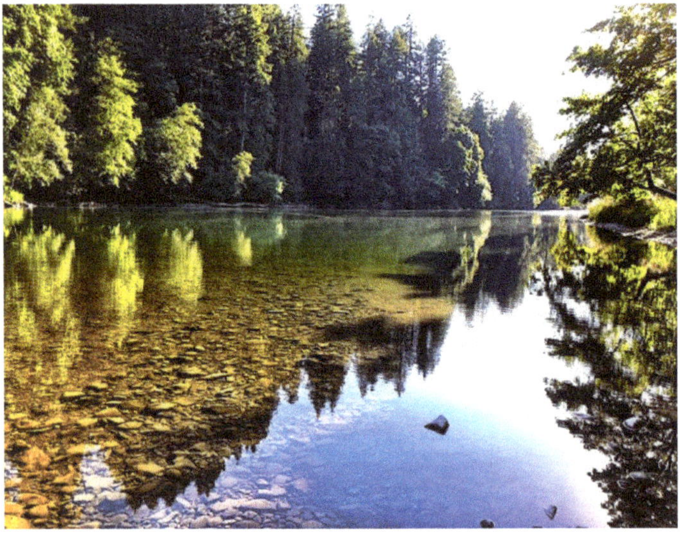

The Lewis River was like glass. Something changed inside and I went home and finished "Mirror-Mirror," an original song. I could feel it. Music was in me again.

Lake Merwin

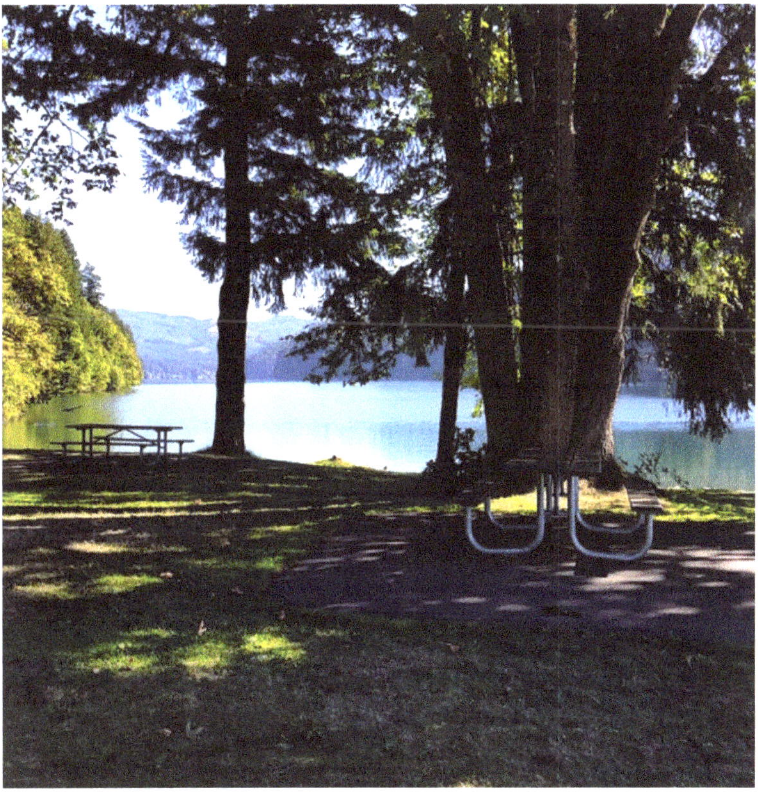

Picnic tables for everyone at Lake Merwin. Great spot for a swim on a hot summer day. I came here as a kid. My folks had their Woodland Washington Class of 1956 Reunion Picnic here. Retro cool.

A local Favorite for boat camping. Merwin Reservoir was formed after the completion of Merwin Dam, in 1931 by the Inland Power and Light Company. The reservoir fluctuates depending on the amount of run-off making boat access difficult at times.

Kokanee are the main target, however, Tiger Muskie planted in 1995 are also popular with anglers. This North Fork Lewis River impoundment located near the town of Ariel, on the south side of Highway SR"503, is shared by Clark and Cowlitz counties.

All Bull Trout and Dolly Varden must be released.

PacifiCorp operates boat launches at Speelyai Bay and Cresap Bay.There is a fee to launch on weekends.Call (800) 547-1501 for updated reservoir levels.

There is very limited shore access.

Two-pole fishing is allowed

Shoreline access: GoodVery limited.

Species you might catch

* Bull trout

* Chinook salmon

* Coho salmon

* Kokanee

* Northern pikeminnow

* Tiger muskie

Lake information

County: Cowlitz

Acreage: 3835.60 ac.Elevation: 242 ft.Center: 45.979477, -122.44844

Source: http://northwestfishingreports.com

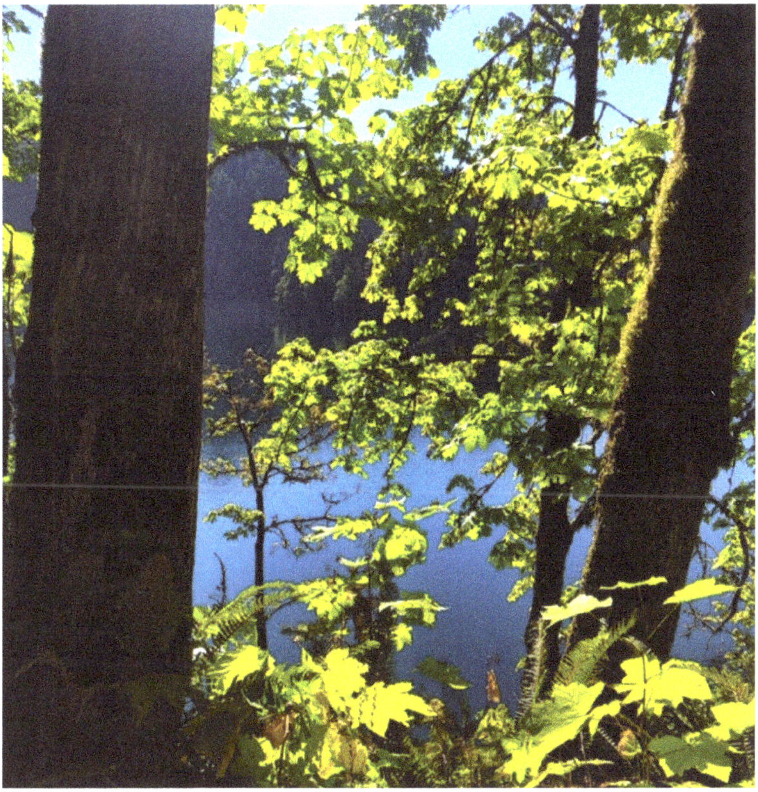

Trail to the Waterfall. Photographers bring your gear.

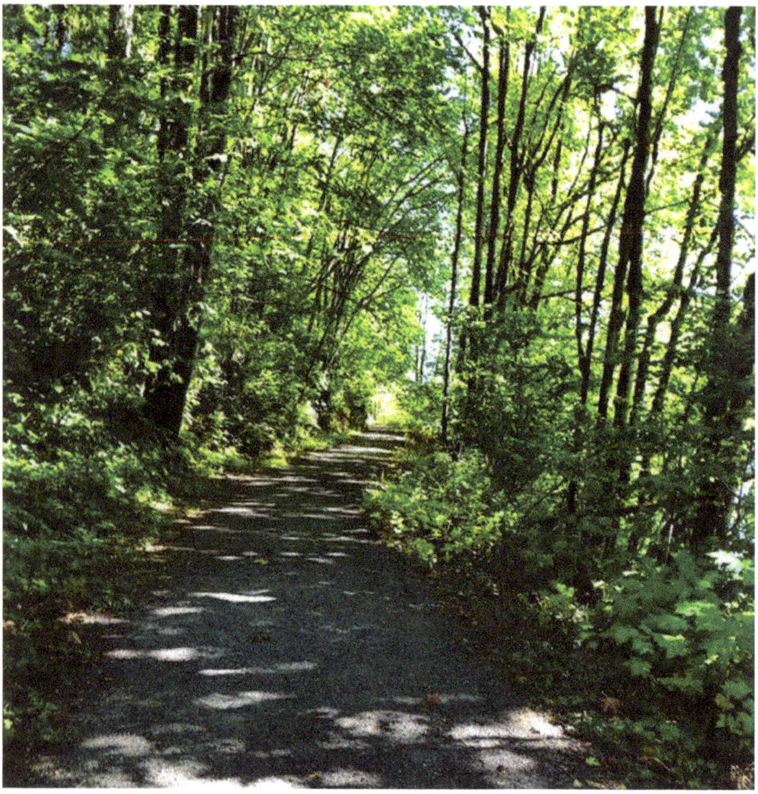

Trail leads to the Waterfall. Wheelchair friendly gravel up to the falls.

Lake Merwin | Ariel. Situated at the confluence of Lewis River and **Lake Merwin**, **Merwin** Park is the largest recreation area along the Lewis River. It's an excellent place to enjoy a picnic, go fishing, play on a playground, and of course, swimming!

Merwin Memories

This place is a kid's dream. The trail above is about a mile and ends with a real live lagoon and a waterfall. I used to come here with my Folks. We attended a 1956 Woodland Class Reunion here. I was just a kid and had a complete blast with my new Friends. Bring a picnic and stay the day. This place is a gem. You will leave with worn out little ones and a smile.

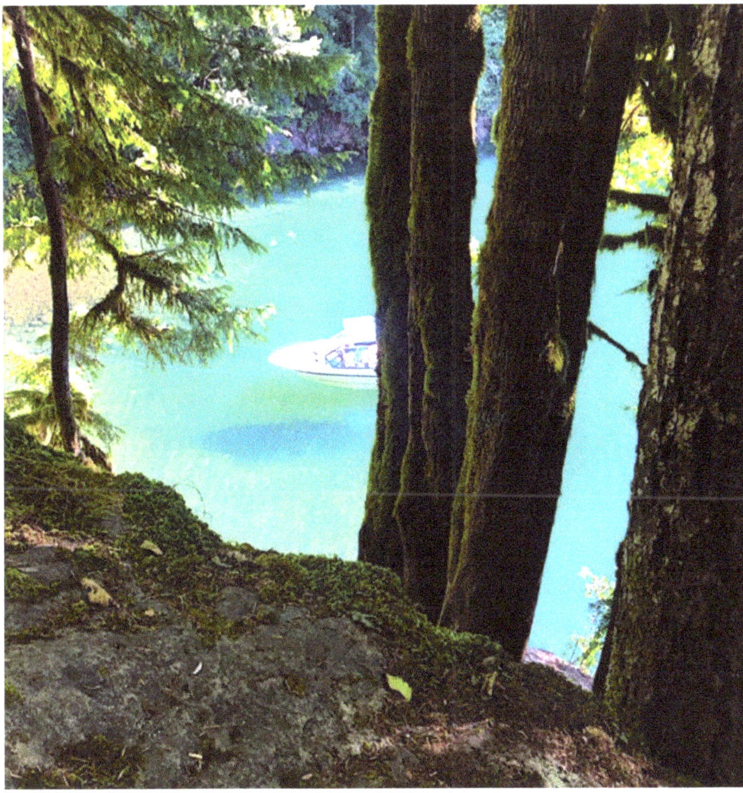

The water is so clear you can see the bottom. This couple were enjoying cheese and Wine.

Speelyai Bay

Speelyai Bay Recreation Area

Speelyai Bay at Lake Merwin is a day use area consisting of 25 picnic tables, parking for 250 vehicles, a two-lane boat ramp and a beach swim area. This Beautiful place is family friendly, clean and a perfect day for the boat and picnic. The swimming area is top knotch and Folks can blanket while they watch the happy swimmers. Winner all the way. It gets crowded on Holidays. Otherwise a Washington State Secret.

Speelyai Bay and Speelyai Creek merges into Lake Merwin (Lewis River) at Lewis River Mile (RM) 29. Speelyai Canal merges into Yale Lake (Lewis River) at Lewis River Mile (RM) 37.5. The mouth of Speelyai Creek is located in T6N R3E, Sections 22/23.

"Speelyai" is a Native American name for their god "Coyote".

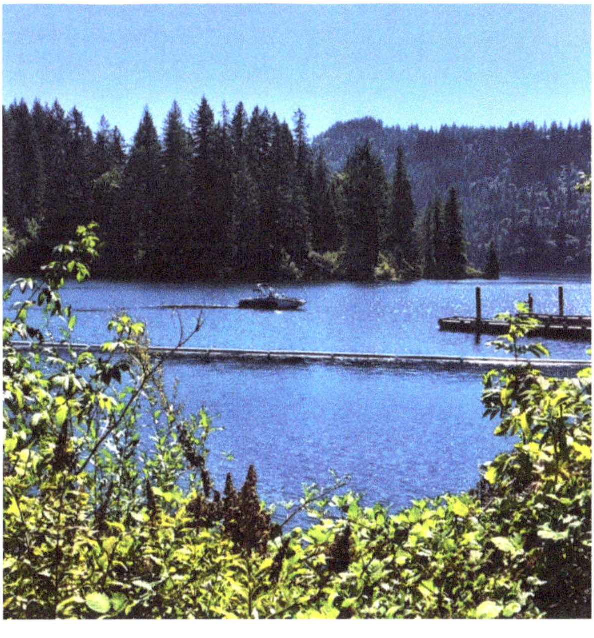

Such a beautiful breezy day at Speelyai Bay that August afternoon.

"**Spilyeh Creek:** a tributary of Lewis River, five miles below the town of Yale, in the southeastern part of Cowlitz County. It was named for an Indian chief of that name. The word means "coyote." (Anna Griffiths, of Yale, in "Names MSS." Letter 243.) In the itinerary of Captain George B. McClellan, 1853, the creek is mentioned with its present name. ("Pacific Railroad Reports," Volume 1., pages 377-389.) The Indians of that vicinity had many legends of "Speelyai" (coyote) the great Indian god. ("Dr. G.P. Kuykendall, in "History of the Pacific Northwest: Oregon and Washington," Volume II, pages 64-66.)" [Edmond S. Meany, 1923, "Origin of Washington Geographic Names"]

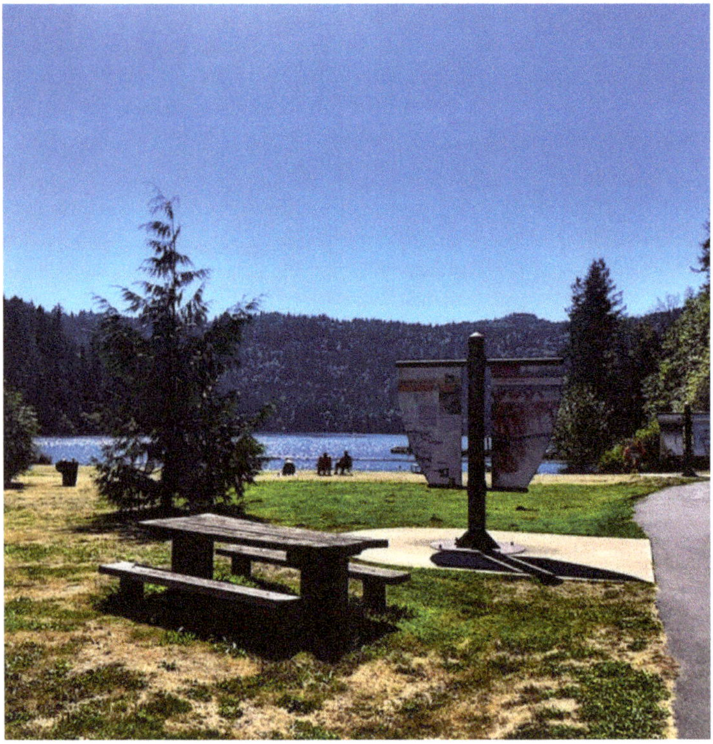

Picnic Tables with a wonderful view of the bay. Informative banners about the history.

"**Speelyai Creek:** The stream of the creek rises south of Merrill Lake, southeast Cowlitz County, flows 10 miles south to Lake Merwin. This is the Indian word for "coyote". In this case, the creek was named for an Indian chief who had adpoted the coyote's name." Hitchman, 1985, "Place Names of Washington"

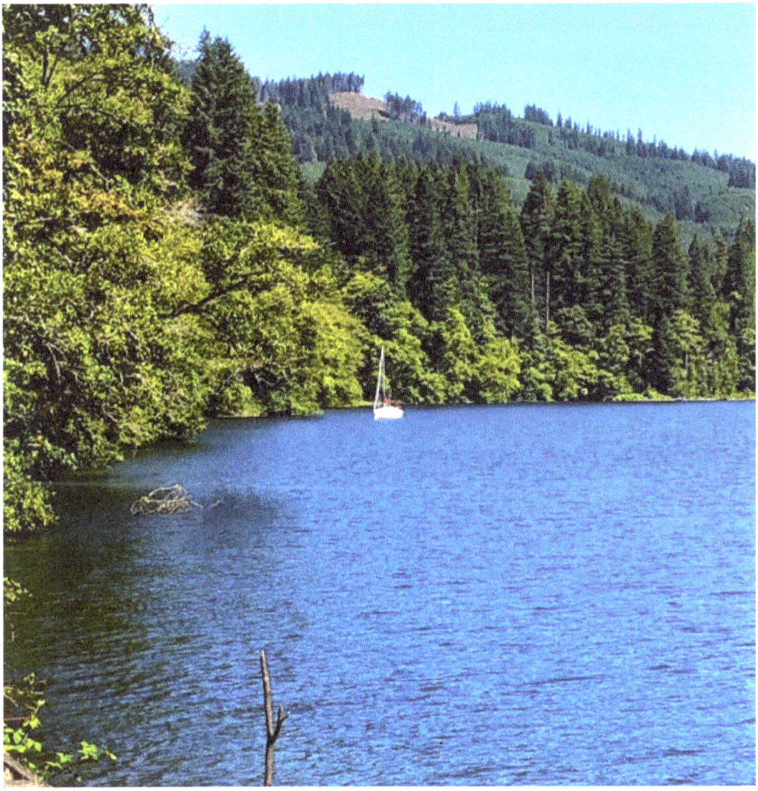

Sailboat takes a rest in the cove. It was a perfect windy and warm.

"**Speelyais Columns:** (Multnomah). These rock columns are on the south bank of the Columbia River near Shepperds Dell. They are the cores of old basalt volcanic vents, the softer coverings of which have been eroded away. They are named with the Indian word *Speelyai*, the name of the coyote trickster of the mid-Columbia region. (*See* Lyman's *Columbia River*, p.8.) The columns were named about 1915 when the Historic Columbia River Highway was completed. In 1999, the compiler was unable to find anyone who could point out their exact location." [McArthur and McArthur, 2003, "Oregon Geographic Names"]

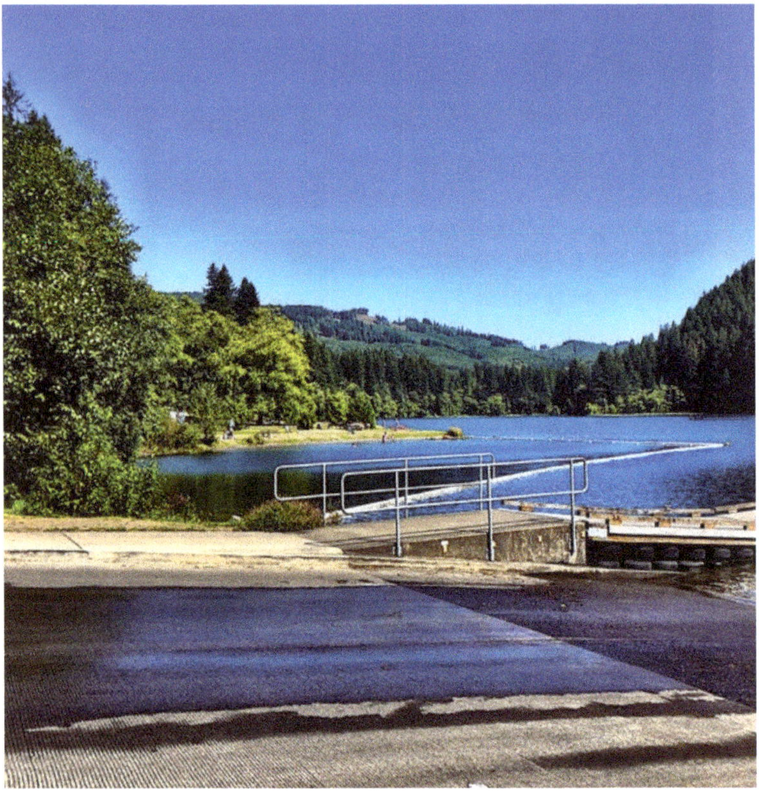

Courteous boaters were quick and efficient with launches. Pacific Northwest forests are filled with wildlife. It is common to hear coyotes howl at night.

SPEELYAI (COYOTE), THE GREAT INDIAN GOD.

An examination into the myths of the Indians shows Coyote as being almost all-powerful, -- transforming the face of nature, changing living beings to stone, transforming himself into a feather, a little mewling baby, or into anything that might forward his purposes. He traveled over the earth, met and subjugated the monsters, demons and tyrant gods that were destroying the people. He always was the friend of the Indian and an enemy to their foes. While he is represented in their mythis as performing such wonderful and supernatural things, he often found himself outwitted and circumvented even by some small and insignificant animal, and is spoken of as doing the most ridiculous and absurd things, and getting into predicaments of the most painful or ludicrous character. He is represented as being very acute and cunning, and as resorting to all sorts of stratagems, fair or unfair, to accomplish his objects. ... In short, Coyote was a being with the qualities of a real coyote and a live Indian. The Indian's god was, in short, like himself, -- full of treachery and deceit, ignorant yet cunning; wise in some respects, yet full of folly and childishness. Upon the whole, Coyote was a pretty good character, viewed from the Indian standpoint, and, in fact, must have represented at one time the Indian's idea of a being worthy to be called god."

Source: Northwest Pacific History Company, 1889, "The Indians of the Pacific Northwest ..., Legends, Myths, Manners and Customs of the Indians": IN: History of the Pacific Northwest: Oregon and Washington ..., Volume II, Chapter LX.

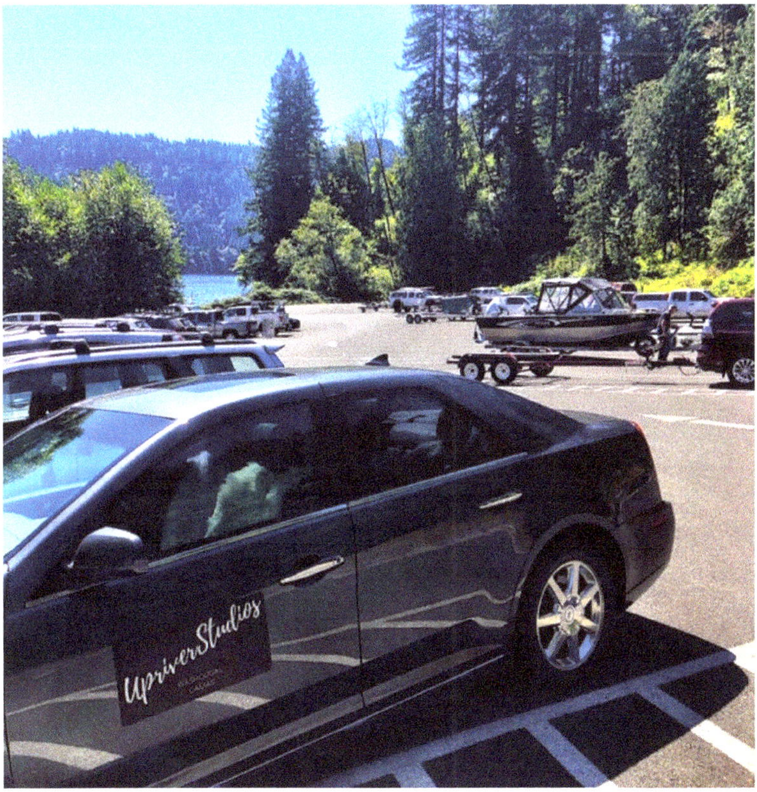

Adventurous couples were swapping travel stories and giving tips for future fun. Great vibe.

Yale Boat Launch

Yale Reservoir was formed after the completion of Yale Dam by Pacific Power and Light in 1953.The main attraction at this reservoir is Kokanee. Although there are four boat ramps on the reservoir, the water level fluctuates making access by boat difficult at times.

This reservoir is located on the North Fork Lewis River. Shallow fishing for kokanee is best in the spring and fall; in the summer months deep fishing is the best method. Coastal Cutthroat Trout can be caught near the mouth of Siouxon Creek.

There are some Bull Trout in the reservoir. **All Bull Trout and Dolly Varden must be released**. PacifiCorp operates all boat launch facilities at Saddle Dam, Yale, Cougar Camp and Beaver Bay. Fees are required to launch on weekends.All ramps may be out of the water when the lake level is lowered. Call (800) 547-1501 for updated reservoir levels.

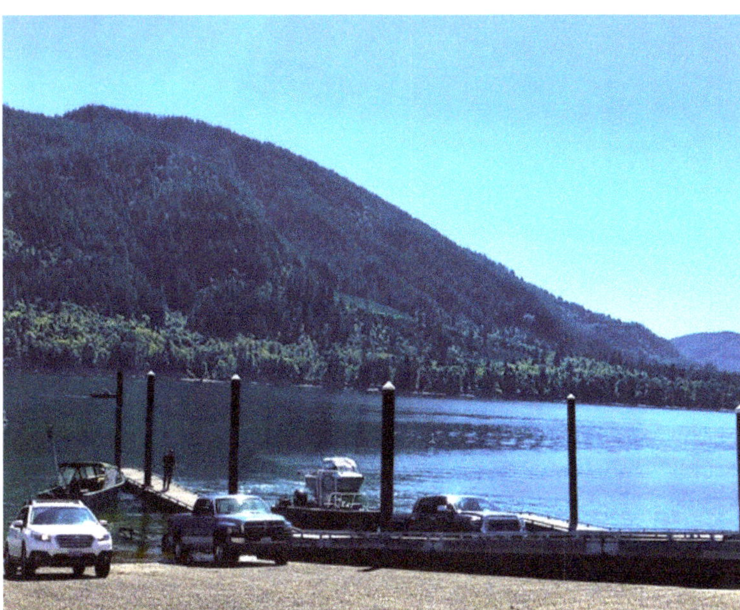

Four lanes of great boat launches. Good trailer parking with restrooms and picnic tables.

Two-pole fishing **is allowed**

Shoreline access: Good
Kokanee fishng is very poor from shore.

Species you might catch

- Bull trout
- Coastal cutthroat trout (resident)
- Kokanee

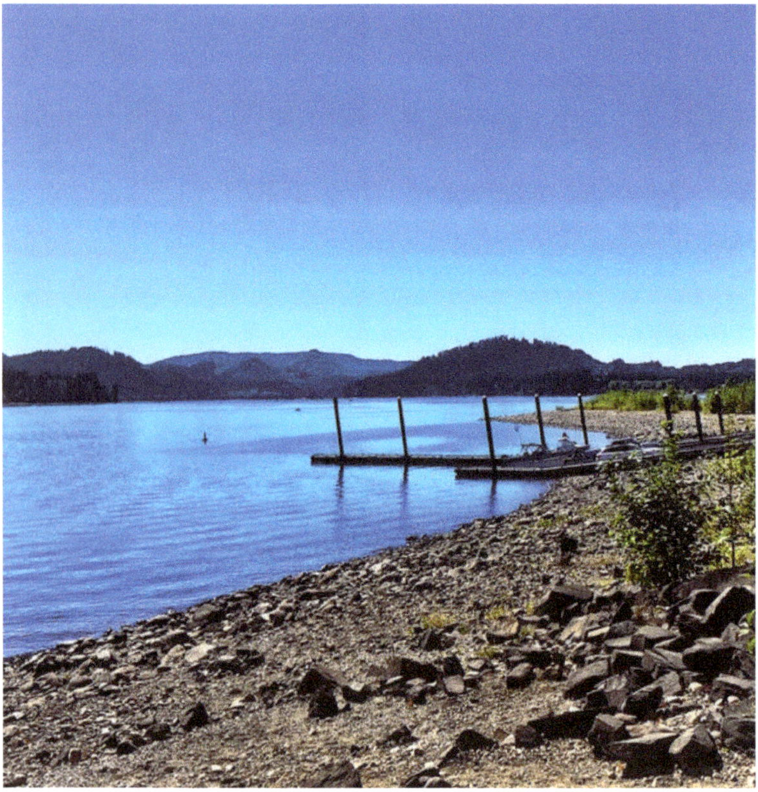

Beautiful August day at Yale. Great launch.

Lake information

County: Cowlitz
Acreage: 3612.10 ac.
Elevation: 486 ft.
Center: 45.99912, -122.320061

Kayak at Yale Lake

By: Matt Klemsz

Kayak before the face of Washington's infamous Mount St. Helens in one of three crystal clear lakes. These calm waters offer kayakers, stand-up-paddle boarders, even swimmers the perfect trip to just get away and enjoy the day!

Just 55 miles northeast of Portland lies a body of water so pure you have to see it to believe it...that's right, we're talking about Yale Lake. One of three lakes beneath Washington's ever rumbling Mount St Helens, Yale offers the outdoor lover just about everything they could ask for: calm waters, forested banks, views of world famous volcanoes...the list goes on and on and on.

Now to begin the journey you obviously need to get there first, and if you're not great with directions you're in luck! After taking exit 22 (Woodland) off I-5 all you have to do is drive 27 miles east on Lewis River Road. The drive is nothing short of picturesque with each twist and turn of the road revealing movie quality views of mountains towering over the lakes.

After those 27 miles you'll find Yale Park to your right, resting midway along the banks of Yale Lake. Open year-round, this park makes for the perfect launch point for a day on the water with a fully functional dual boat launch as well as sand and rocky banks (a much more preferred method when it comes to casting off your kayak).

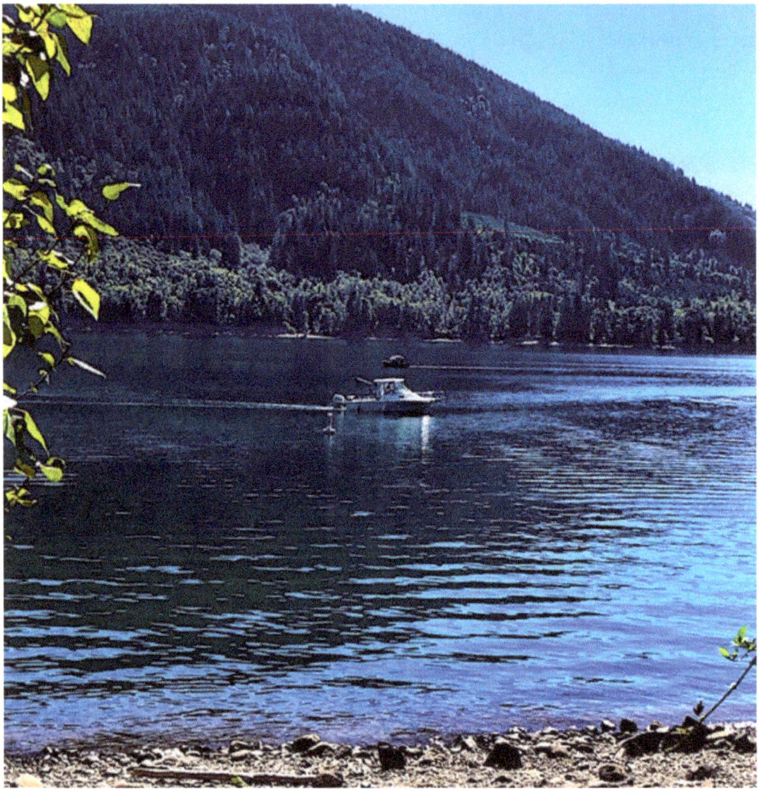

Boaters exploring the beauty. A peaceful afternoon.

As soon as you hit the water the entire world is yours, and with 7.5 miles of water to explore there's truly no other place like it. You can paddle for as short or as long as you wish. If you're feeling extra adventurous, bring a fishing pole and see if you can sink a line or two! And hey... take a glance over your shoulder occasionally and you may just see that infamous peak looming over head.

What are you waiting for?! Grab the GoPro, life jackets, kayaks and snacks and head on out there!! Source: theoutofbound.com Special Thanks to Matt Klemsz

Swift Reservoir

Swift Reservoir is located twenty-eight miles northeast of Woodland, on the south side of Forest Road 90. A public boat launch at Swift Forest Camp, managed by PacifiCorp, has two concrete ramps. There is a fee to launch on weekends. When the reservoir is drawn down, the water level drops below the end of the launch. Call PacifiCorp at (800) 547-1501 for reservoir level information.

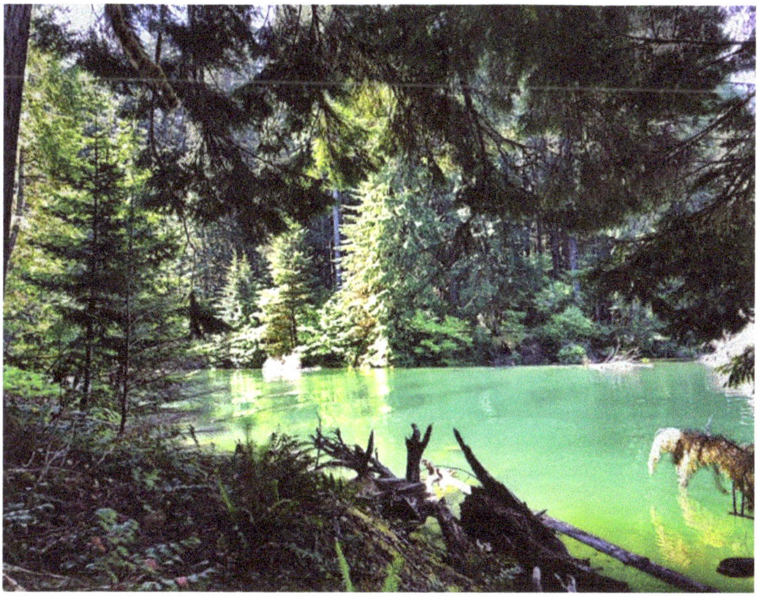

Boat camping at Swift is fantastic, This late afternoon the sun lit up the lagoon and it turned a brilliant green until sunset.

During April and May fish tend to congregate near the dam and around streams entering the reservoir. By June, trout should be dispersed throughout the reservoir. Landlocked salmon rules apply with a 15" maximum size on salmon.

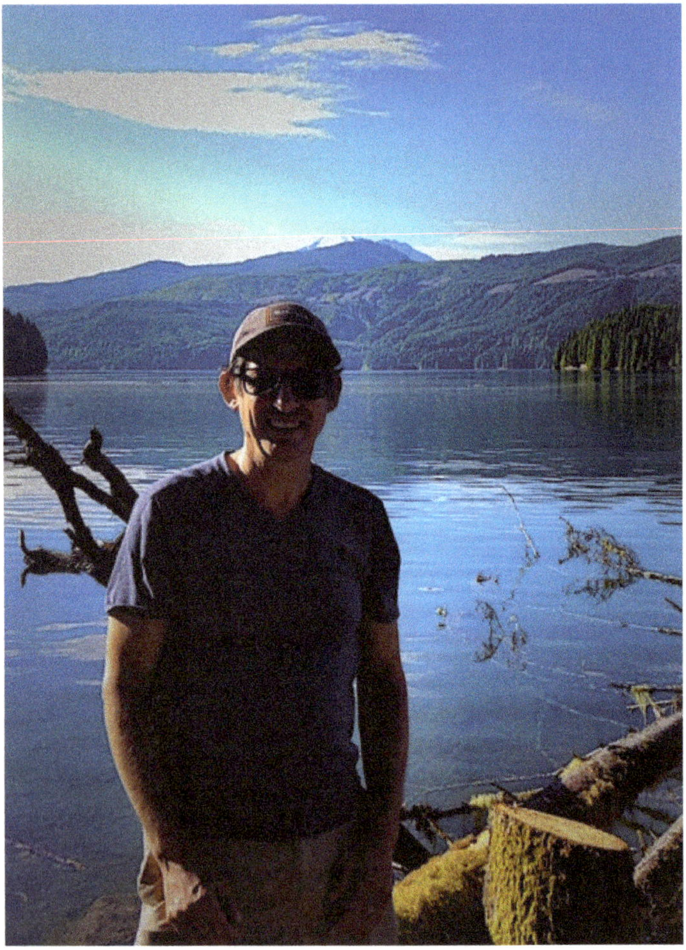

Darold takes in a summer day at Swift. The weather was perfect.

Selective gear rules are in effect in the upper portion of the reservoir; check the regulation pamphlet for boundaries.

Shore access is limited. Shore access is available along the campground and below Eagle Cliff Bridge.

All bull trout and Dolly Varden must be released.

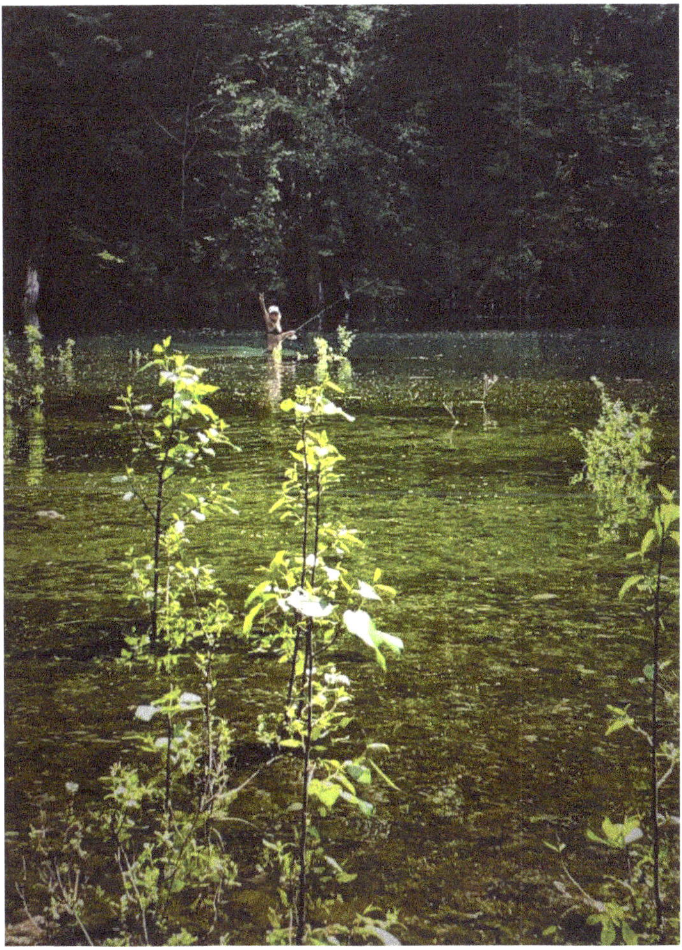

Ready with a picnic, Sister Jody Fishing Swift.

Species you might catch

- Bull trout
- Coho salmon
- Rainbow trout

Lake information

County: Skamania
Acreage: 4585.40 ac.
Elevation: 1012 ft.
Center: 46.054388, -122.110115

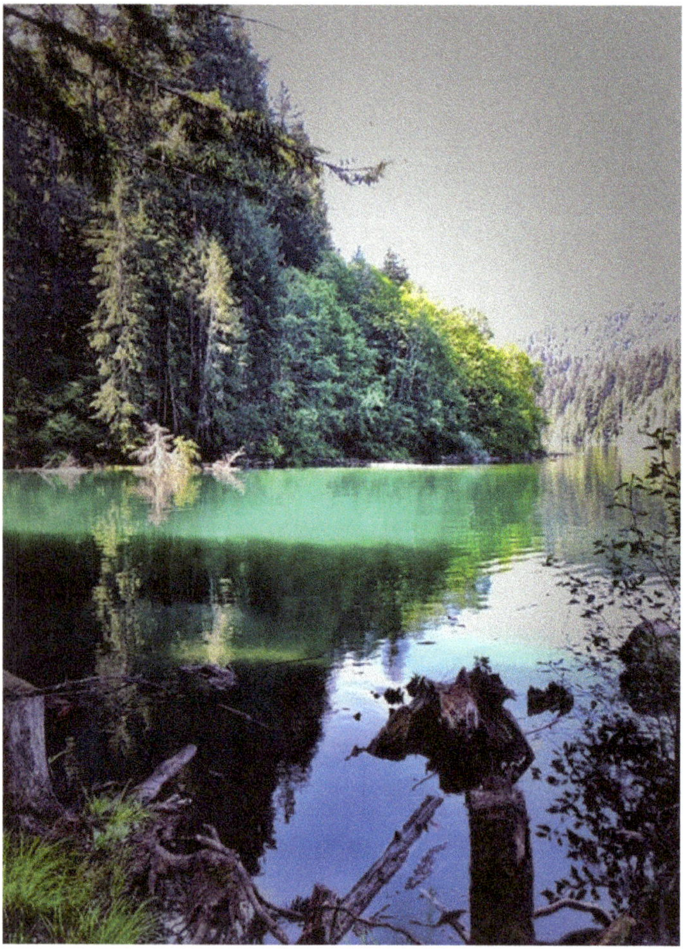

Boat camping Swift Reservoir Washington State.

Celebrating Brother Dan's Birthday during the "2020 Pandemic." Boat camping and fishing Swift, Dan gave us a camp tour and showed us the old growth trees. We had lunch, picked fresh blackberries and found mushrooms in the woods. After lunch we took the boat out trolling and looking for waterfalls.

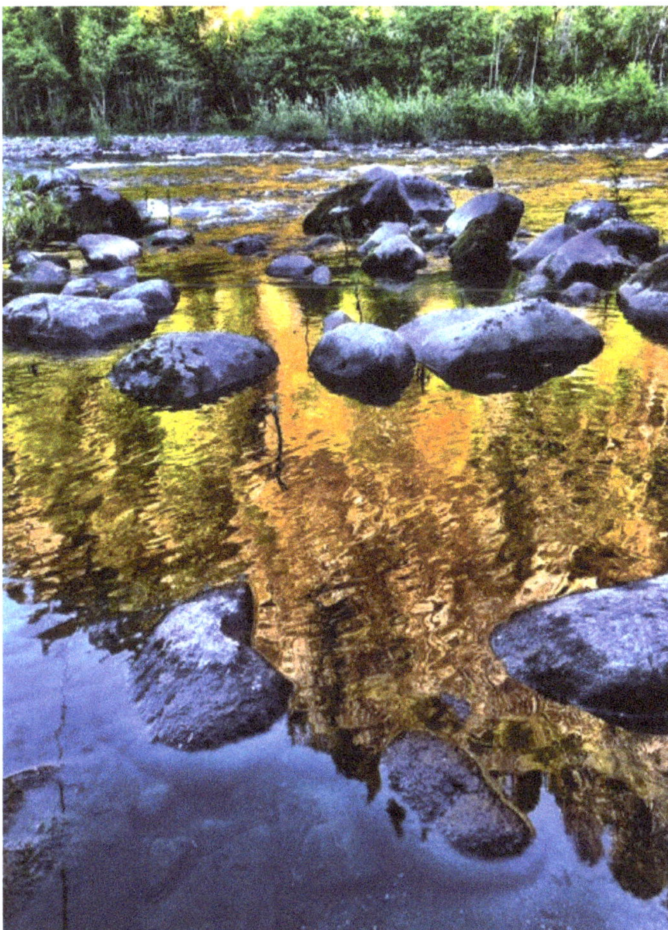

Darold caught two fish here in about 20 miniutes. We had a great day.

The stunning beauty of Swift speaks for itself. It has been a family tradition to camp at Swift Reservoir for many Pacific Northwest homegrown natives. When you live here you need not drive for days to see awe inspiring scenery. The old growth trees are breathtaking. Thick ancient forest has a smell only hikers know. Always good fishing and a photographers dream. Very few camp boat camp spots. Be prepared. We had the most wonderful visit. Memories are so good when gathered together and kept close to the heart. This is one of those days I will look back upon as an elder.

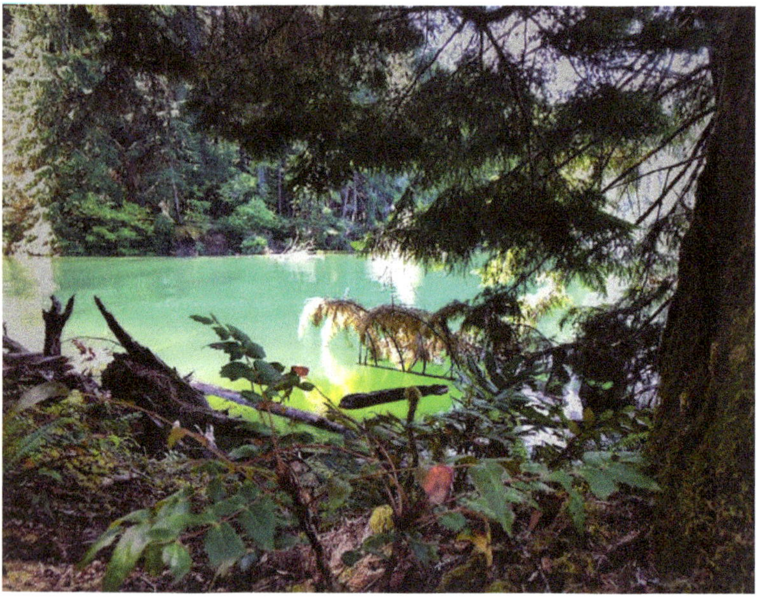

Late evening sun made the water seem to light up. Good times.

Merrill Lake

Merrill Lake was formed when lava flows from Mt. St. Helens blocked the stream valley. In the early 1930's the lake was planted with Eastern Brook Trout, Rainbow Trout and Yelowstone Cutthroat. Brown Trout were introduced in 1987 and have proved to be very successful.

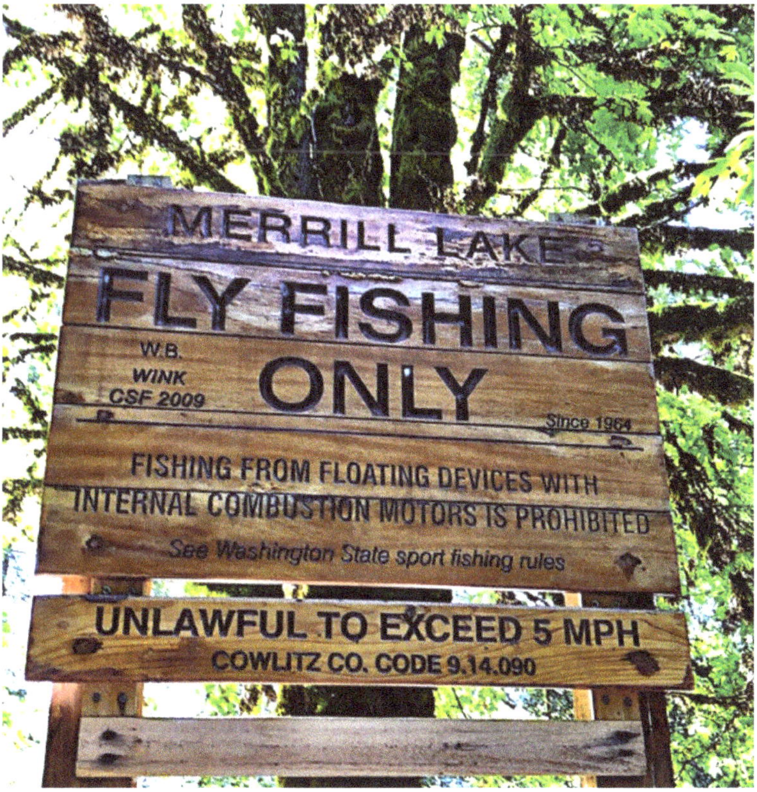

Bring your fly pole. Legend has it, there have been Bigfoot sightings in the area. The annual D.B Cooper party used to be a real hoot at the old Ariel Tavern. Back in the day my Band played some wild blow-outs there.

This fly-fishing, catch-and-release-only lake is located north of Cougar near Mount St. Helens. It is open to fishing year-round, but action is usually slow and often inaccessible during the winter months due to snow. Merrill contains Coastal Cutthroat, Brown Trout to several pounds and some Rainbow Trout.

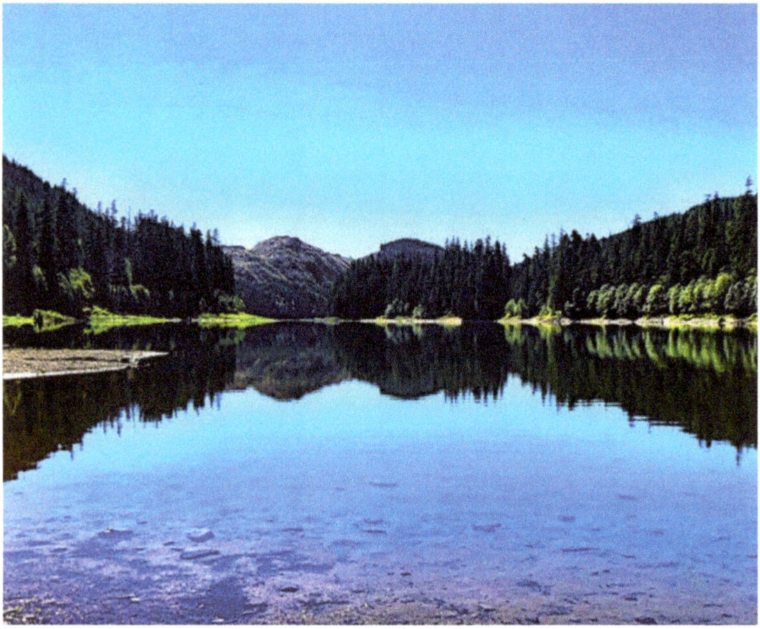

Time seems to stand still in places like this. It's really cool to know so many generations have enjoyed the lakes harvest.

The lake was stocked in 2018 with catchable Rainbow Trout.

Two-pole fishing **is NOT allowed**

Special fishing restrictions:

- **Fly fishing only for this lake**

Shoreline access: Good
Shore access is available as the water level drops during the spring.

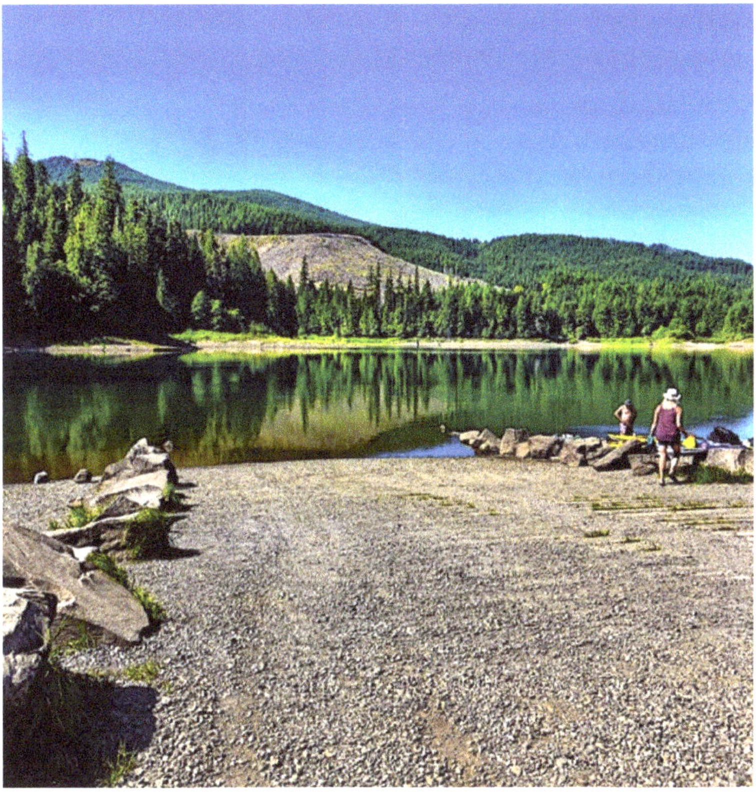

Not many camp spots but I think that's the idea.

Species you might catch

- Brook trout
- Brown trout
- Coastal cutthroat trout (resident)
- Rainbow trout

Lake information

County: Cowlitz
Acreage: 283.40 ac.

Elevation: 1524 ft.
Center: 46.094333, -122.324233

This 114-acre site consists of a forest cover of mixed conifers and hardwoods along a lake at the 1,550-foot elevation. Merrill Lake NRCA is prime habitat for birds of prey, including osprey and bald eagles, and is also home to waterfowl such as bufflehead, common goldeneye, and hooded merganser.

A regionally popular catch-and-release fly fishing spot, Merrill Lake has a boat launch for small craft (non-gasoline powered) and a nine-site campground. Spring through fall camping—on a first-come first-served basis—is mostly walk-in from the main parking area, with a few sites accessible by vehicle.

Features Protected: Old-growth forest, mid-elevation lake, Cascade torrent salamander, osprey, bald eagle
Ecoregion: West Cascades (Cowlitz County)

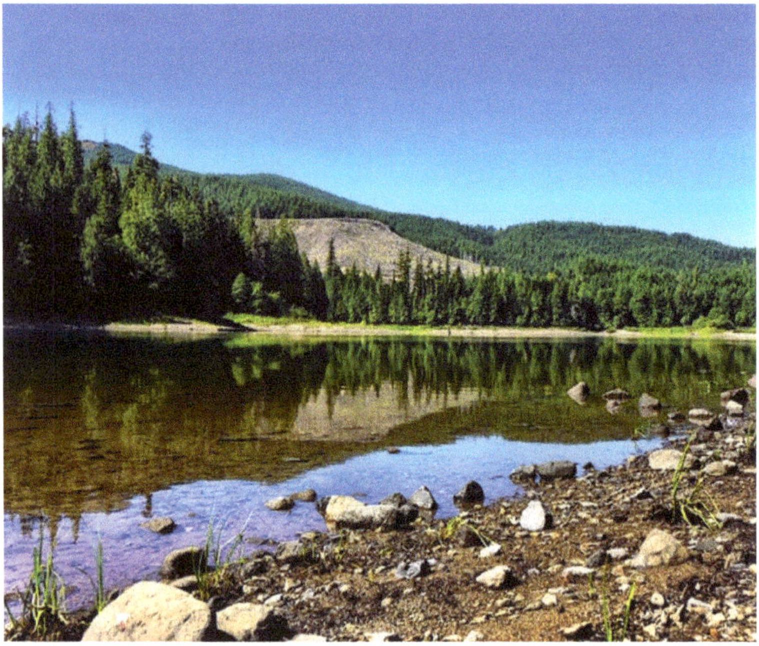

Merrill Lake near Cougar Washington Early September. Merrill is Fly fishing only.

Science, Research and Monitoring

Public and private universities, other research institutions and individual researchers may contact DNR to propose a research project at the site. If you are interested in pursuing research at Merrill Lake NRCA, please contact David Wilderman, natural areas ecologist, at david.wilderman@dnr.wa.gov.

Environmental Education and Public Access

Low-impact Recreation Sites

Merrill Lake Campground

Merrill Lake Campground has a 1-mile nature trail with interpretive signs in an old Douglas fir/western hemlock forest. Campground includes toilet facilities, campsites, parking and boat launch. Merrill Lake is a catch-and-release fly-fishing lake. For more information, contact the DNR Pacific Cascade Region natural areas manager.

Recreation alert: Campground and Day-use Areas are closed due to fire in area.

- Dogs allowed on leash.
- Garbage service is not provided. Pack out what you pack in.
- Enjoy campfires in approved fire pits in designated campgrounds only. Check for burn bans.
- Don't Move Firewood: Help protect Pacific Northwest forests by preventing the spread of invasive species. Firewood can carry insects and diseases that can threaten the health of our western forests. Please purchase firewood near your campsite. Find more information here.
- Campground **closed seasonally from Nov. 15 - May 12.**

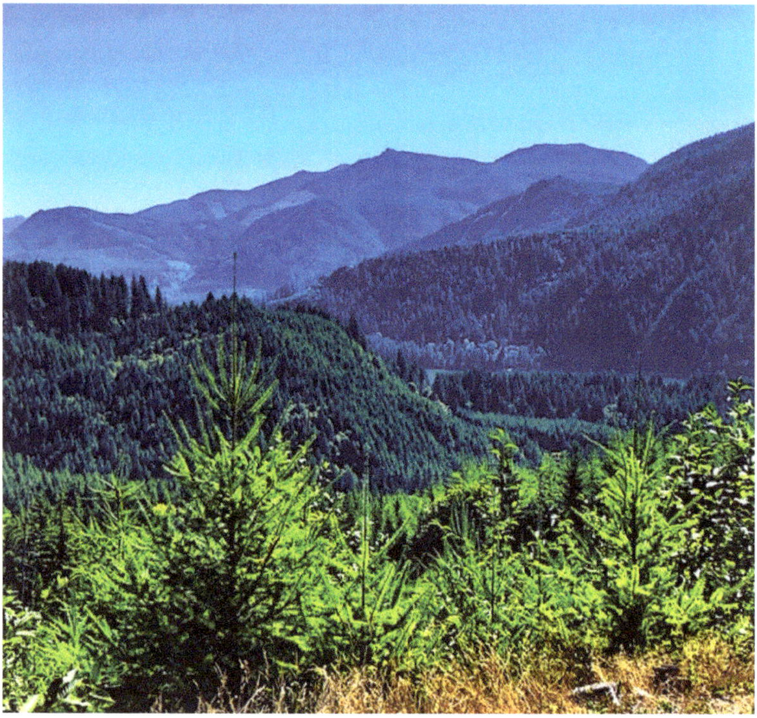

The road to Merrill Lake is perfectly rugged. Don't bring the low-rider.

Directions to the Site

From Woodland, take Highway 503 east and travel about 27 miles; before reaching the town of Cougar, turn left onto USFS Road 81 (you'll see a sign for Merrill Lake and Kalama Horse camp) and travel north about 3.5 miles; the campground access road will be on the left.

A Washington State Discover Pass is required for parking at this site. This funding helps DNR manage these important natural areas across the state.

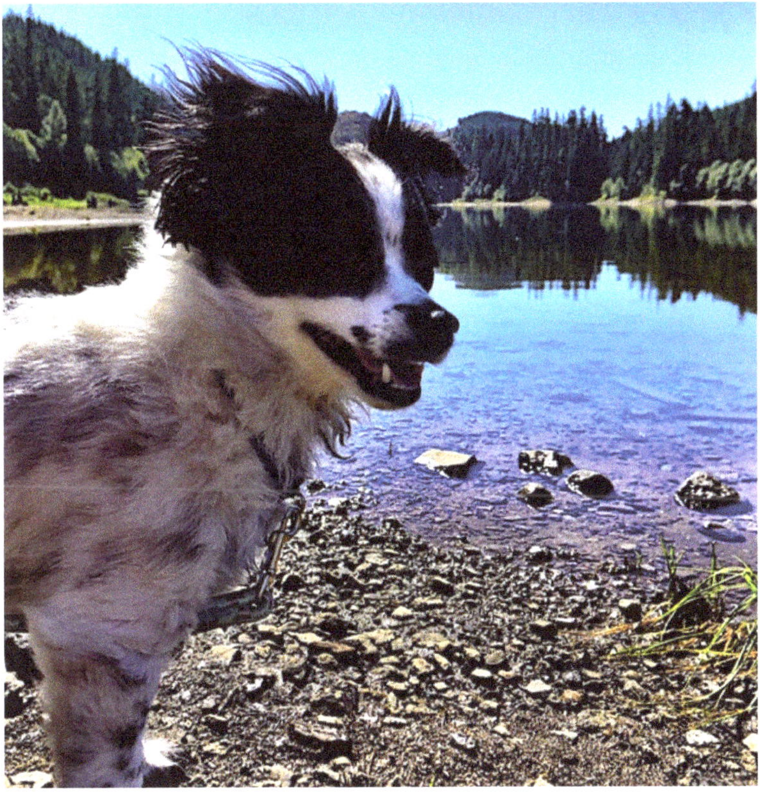

Buddy Love travels on all photography & fishing trips and is an avid camper.

Fly Fishing Oasis

What a beautiful place. Quiet, picturesque scene. The Lake was calm. A few folks were camping and enjoying the lake to themselves. Only a few camp spots making it the ideal getaway for the fly fisherman. The now famous Ape Caves, 16 miles up the Forest Service Road 81. Campgrounds in Cougar and Beaver Bay. I would suggest going on a summer weekday. "Oh.....and you didn't hear any of this from me." Enjoy.

Moulton Falls

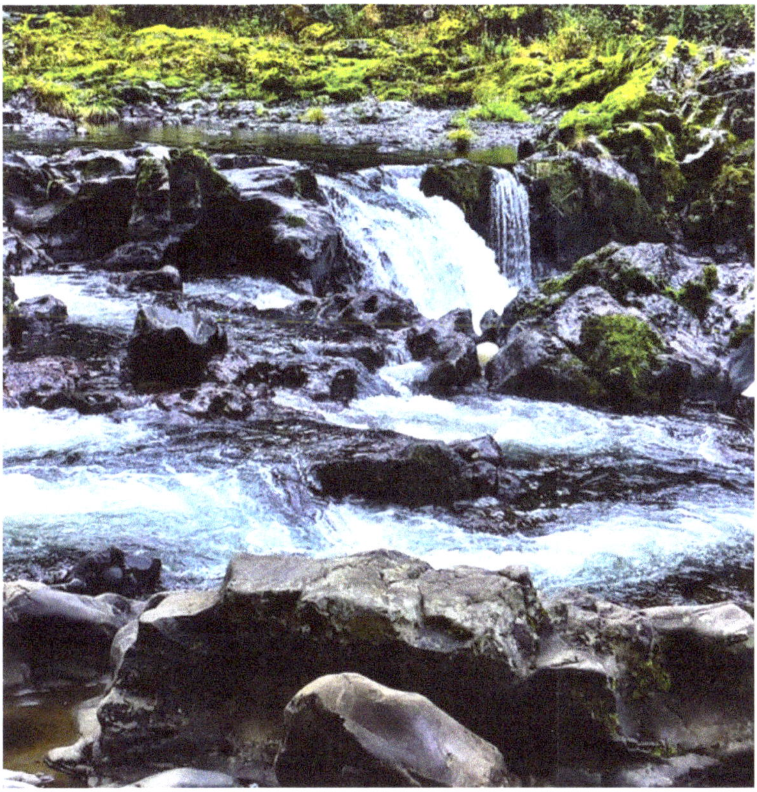

Moulton Falls in Washington State.

Lesser known than the waterfalls of the Columbia River Gorge, the picturesque Moulton Falls offers a scenic day trip free from the typical crowds of waterfall chasers and selfie takers.

To discover this hidden gem, take a 40-minute drive from downtown Vancouver along the Northern Clark County Scenic Drive. The 387-acre park, at the confluence of the East Fork of the Lewis River and Big Tree Creek, features two waterfalls and a wooden arch footbridge more than three stories high. The collection of deep pools is an amazing escape from the summer heat and a popular cliff jumping spot.

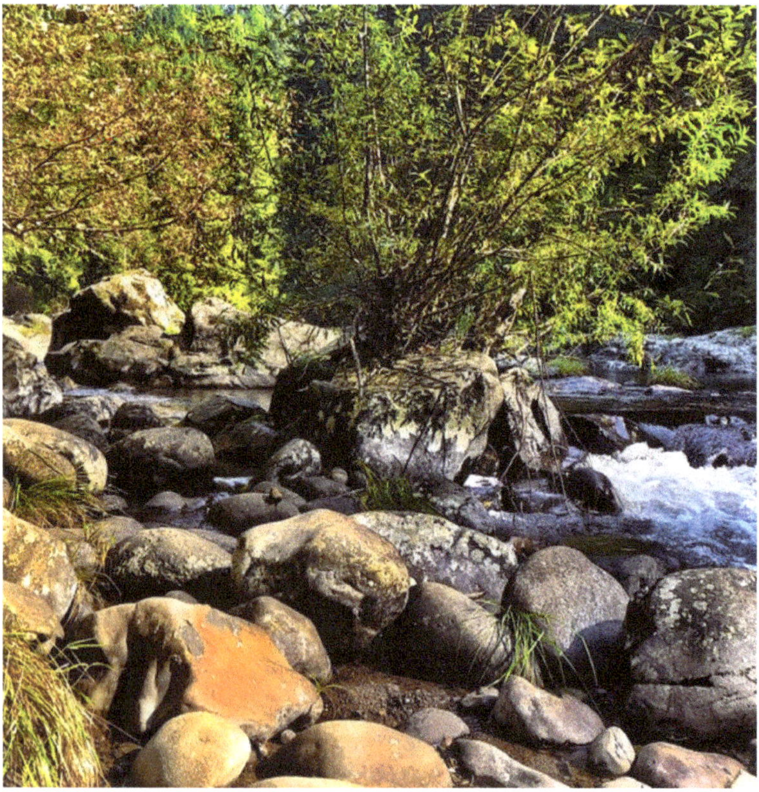

Lewis River feeds the Moulton Falls. Lewis River is a tributary to the Columbia River.

Heavily forested on both sides of the river, the Moulton Falls Trail guides hikers of all skill levels four miles out-and-back along the river. For more experienced explorers, find the starting spot to the longer and steeper Bells Mountain Trail approximately a quarter of a mile downriver from the bridge.

The Chelatchie Prairie Railroad excursion train also passes through Moulton Falls Park, and areas of interest include volcanic rock formations from early lava flows, historic Indian meeting grounds, and a swing bridge on Big Tree Creek. Source: visitvancouverusa.com

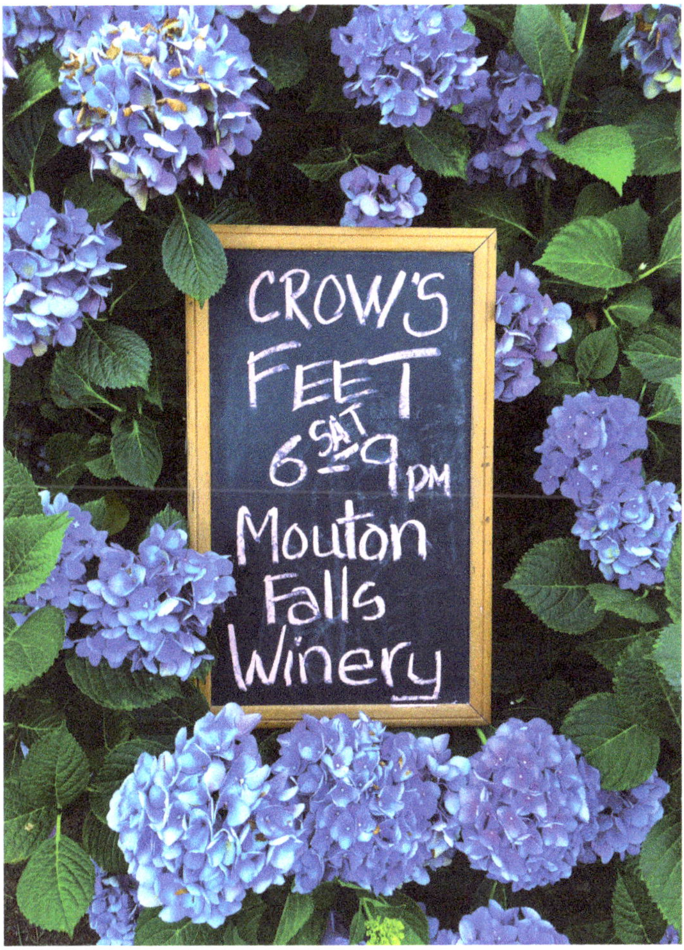

Crow's Feet Band is a duo. I play live music with Twig Sullivan. Our shows are at Local pubs and wineries. Yes, Portland Friends, we play all the way up there! #crowsfeetband

Hiking Moulton Falls

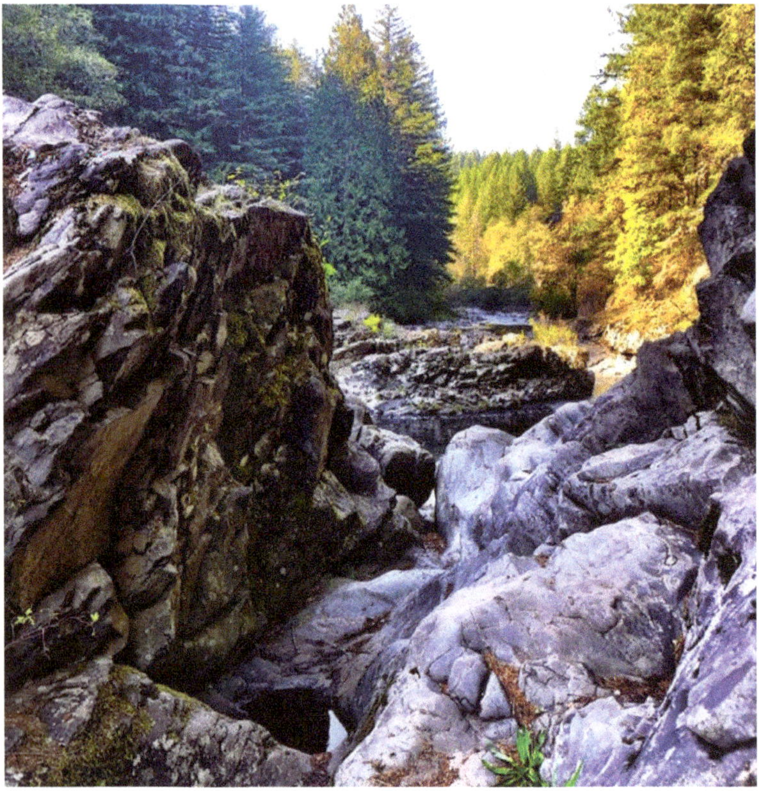

The river has cut a gorge through the earth. Moulton lava rocks are smooth from years of racing waters.

Moulton Falls Trail is an out-and-back hike along the Lewis River. The trail crosses a picturesque footbridge and then follows the Lewis River with the river to the right and a mossy cliff to the left. The wide hard-surfaced trail is mostly flat, making this a perfect year round hike for people of all ages.

This hike combines a peaceful stroll with a bit of adventure. After a short steep pitch down from the parking lot, the virtually flat trail allows you to cruise down the spacious path as fast or a slow as you like. For a side adventure, you can check out Big Tree Falls or climb the Bells Mountain Trail to a viewpoint.

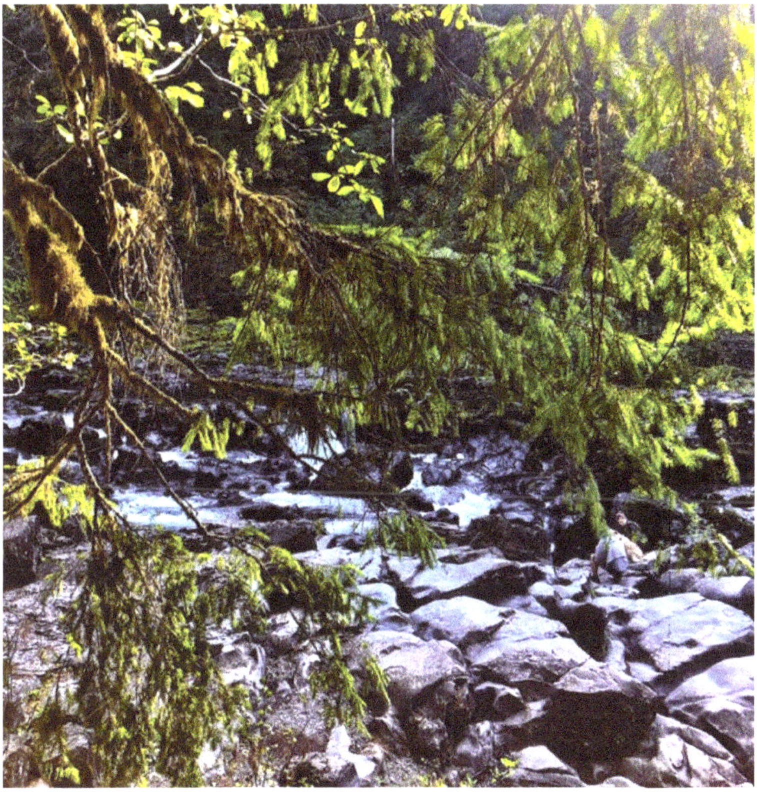

It's like a place they would have filmed a Star Trek episode. The volcanic lava gives it a unearthly feel.

The drive to the trailhead follows part of the Clark County Scenic Drive and is worth the trip alone. The road follows a particularly beautiful stretch of the Lewis River as it flows over volcanic rock formations. The smooth rocks and small pools make this a favorite summertime place for locals to swim and sun. The road also passes the not-to-be-missed Lucia Falls. It is definitely worth stopping and taking the short walk to view one of the region's most scenic water features.

The hike starts at the Moulton Falls overflow parking lot near the junction of Lucia Falls Road with Sunset Falls Road. There are multiple paths in this area, so make sure to snap a photo of the map at the trailhead if you don't have a map with you.

From the parking lot, turn left at the trailhead sign and go down the slope towards the river. Partway down the hill, you will come to a junction with a path leading off to the right. You will go left for this hike, but this is a good place to take a side trip to the right and go see Moulton falls.

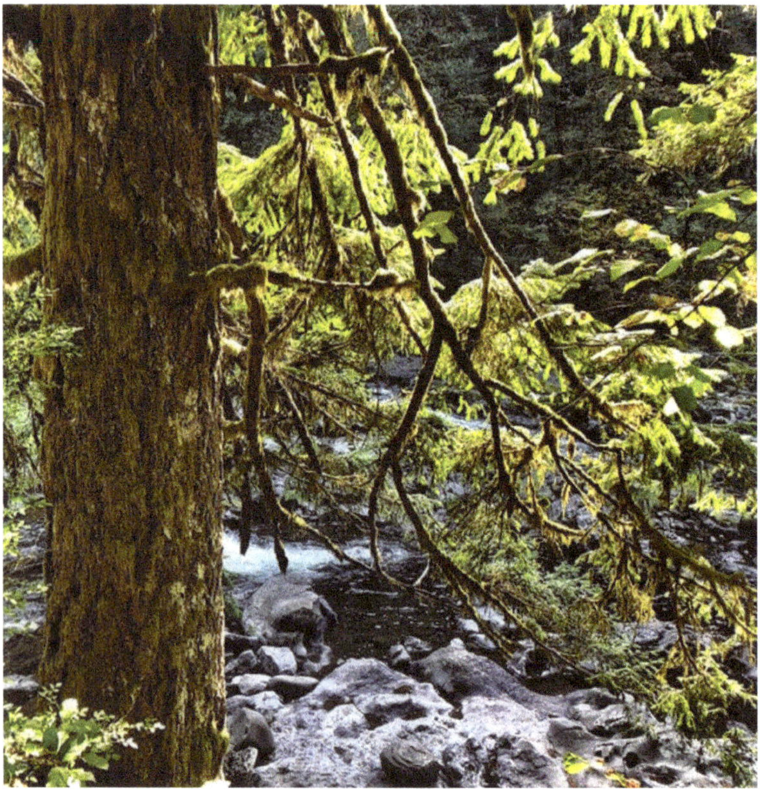

Old growth trees line the road. Lava riverbanks.

After you return to the trail, continue downhill to the arch bridge with its spectacular views of the Lewis River far below. On one side, the river flows through a narrow tree-lined canyon, and on the other side the river opens up to peacefully flow towards the falls. This is the best spot on the hike to take postcard-perfect pictures, so be sure to stop, enjoy the view, and take some photos.

Just after the crossing the bridge, you will come to two junctions to the right leading to picnic areas. Keep left and stay on the wide path that follows an old road grade along the river through a mixed forest of big leaf maples, alders, cedars and Douglas firs. Although there is a road across the river, it is mostly hidden from view with the river masking the road sounds.

A half mile from the trailhead, you will come to the Bells Mountain Trail. If you are feeling energetic, you may want to take a side excursion to a viewpoint 1.5 miles up the trail. This rigorous 1,000-foot climb will certainly earn you bragging rights if you decide to tackle it.

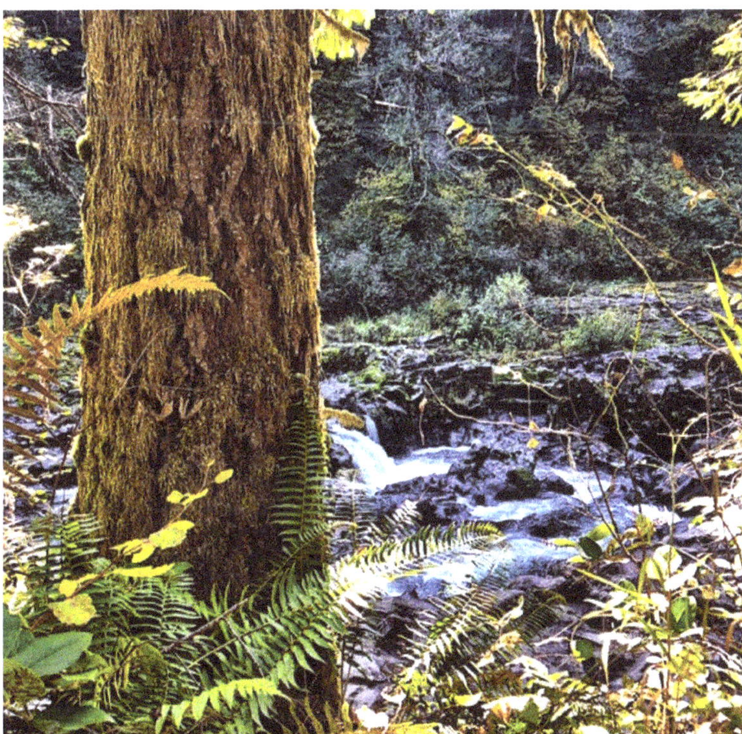

Moulton Falls is an interesting place to see. Perfect day trip.

Our hike, however, continues on the main trail along the river. In about a mile, the path leaves the river to follow the Chelatche Prairie Railroad to a small lake with a picnic area on the far end. This is a pleasant spot for a snack or picnic and is the turnaround point for this hike. If you would like a longer hike or need toilet facilities, you can go a half mile further to the Hantwick Road trailhead. After you turn around, retrace your steps back to your car.

Before you leave, be sure to cross Lucia Falls Road and follow the trail to Big Tree Falls. These impressive Niagra-like falls are the best of the three in the park.

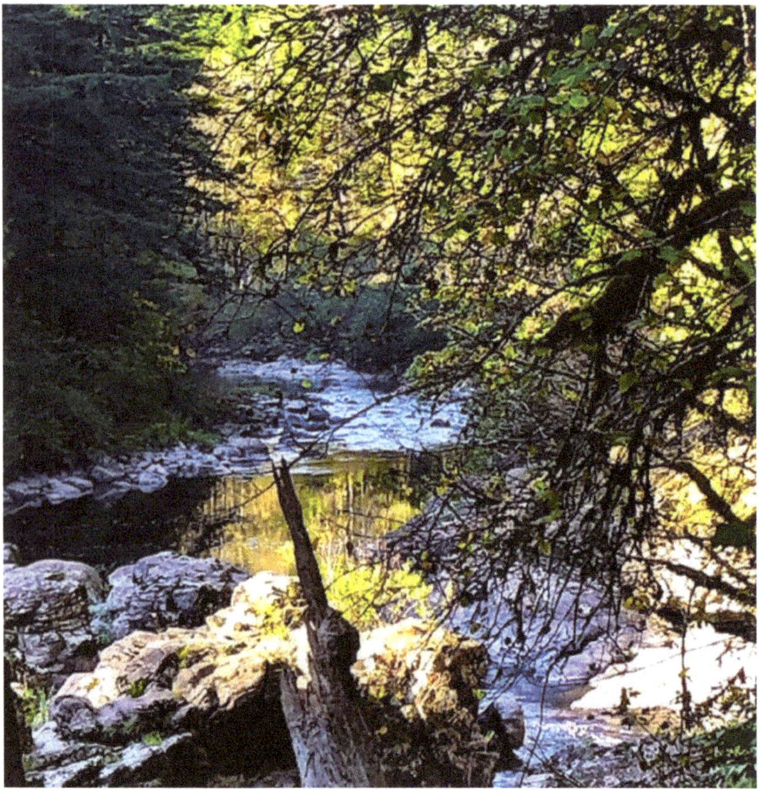

October the leaves start to put on their yearly show. Fish are running the river.

When the steel bridge just below the falls is open, you can get striking views of the water as it churns through a narrow chasm beneath you. If the bridge is open, you can turn your trek into a 1.7 mile loop. Otherwise, turn around and return to your car.

WTA Pro Tip: After the hike, consider stopping at one of the local wineries, soaking your feet in one of the pools along the river, or stopping at Rocky's Pizza in Battle Ground for food in an eclectic old-west setting.

Source: wta.org

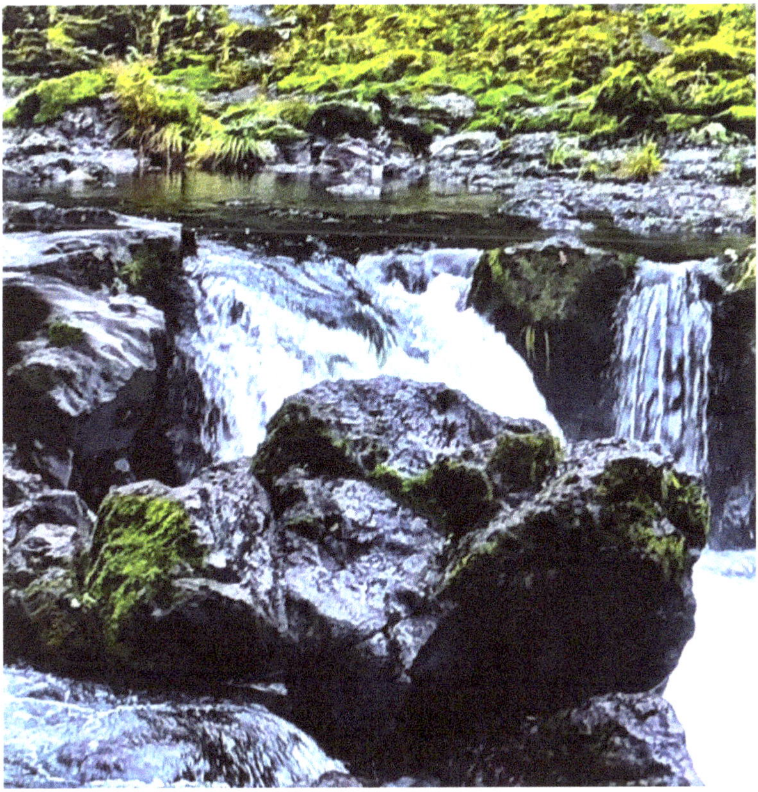

Highly recommend going on a week day. My count was 15 parking spots. No matter where you are coming from, it is a beautiful drive. Beware there are tire spikes on the parking lot exit. Parking is free. Dogs on a leash. Photographers enjoy!

Pacific Northwest Forests

Originally claimed by Spain, Britain, Russia, and finally the United States, the Northwest was jointly occupied by Britain and the United States until 1846, when the 49th parallel was made the boundary between the United States and British-held Canada. The area had been explored by Meriwether Lewis and William Clark in 1804–06 and by various trappers and fur traders, and settlers began arriving there by way of the Oregon Trail in the 1840s. Farming and trapping were the original economic mainstays, to be followed in later years by lumbering, fishing, and mining.

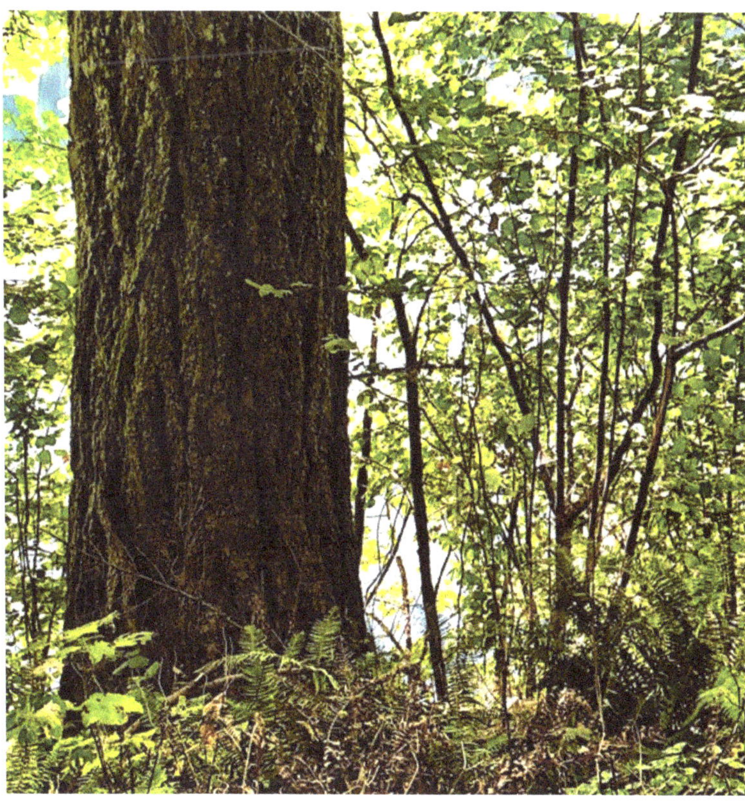

The power hits you if you pay attention and listen to the forest.

A region of spectacular beauty and valuable natural resources, the Northwest has attracted relatively few immigrants largely because of its basically wet climate. Furthermore, the economy has tended to rely on a few big industries, such as timber, and aeronautics in Washington, so that fluctuations in the business cycle are particularly severe in the region.

Growth rates in the Northwest have been high but generally below those of neighbouring states in the Southwest. Government has tended to be progressive and especially sensitive to environmental issues.

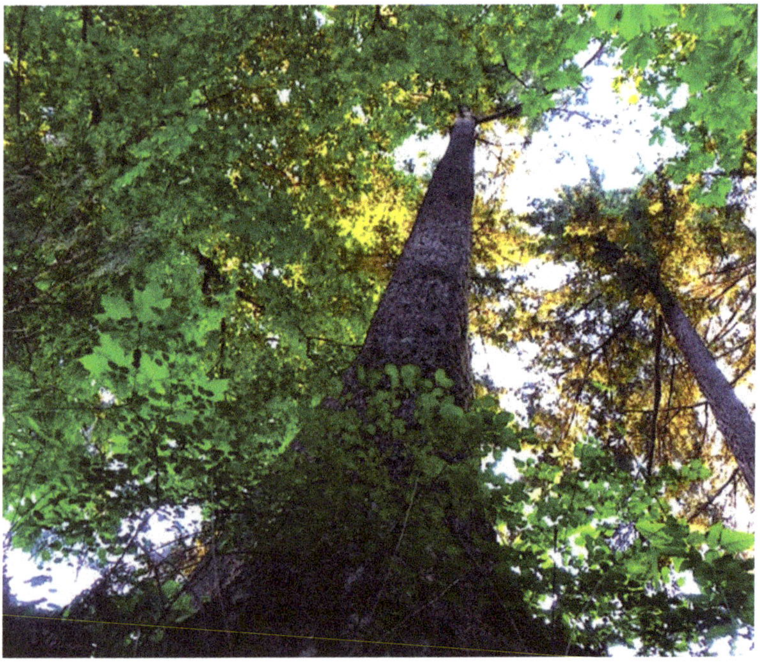

"We are the keepers of our own peace." -Elizabeth Rhodes Moffett- 1986

If you have ever run through the deep woods as a child, I don't have to explain the heaven on earth it deeply is. The smell when a rain starts to nourish it's majestic creation and the smell is immeasurable. "Get yourself deep in the trees," is a line in one of my original songs about prediction and self healing. If you go to the woods and sit for a while. The forest will start to talk to you. Animals will reveal themselves to you and birds will tattle you out. It's simply glorious. The smell never leaves your brain and you can recall it often. I think the elders knew where the true peace lived. In the deep woods of the forest. Culinary treasures abound. It's perfect for meditation. It makes us realize how small we truly are.

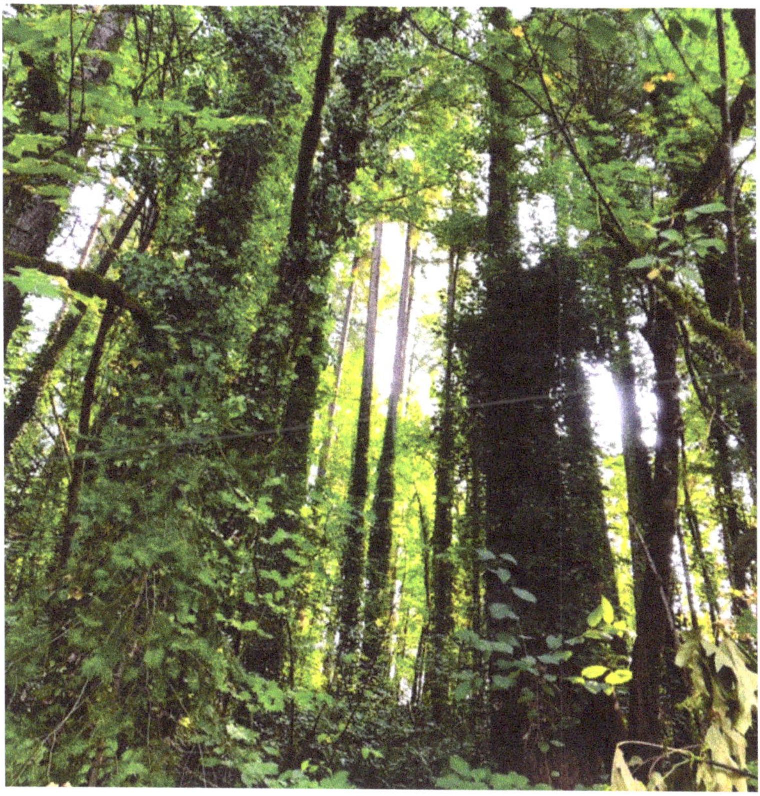

Running through the deep woods on a trail is a childhood memory. Nothing else like the smell of the slightly damp earth and the way the air is beginning to feel October cold.

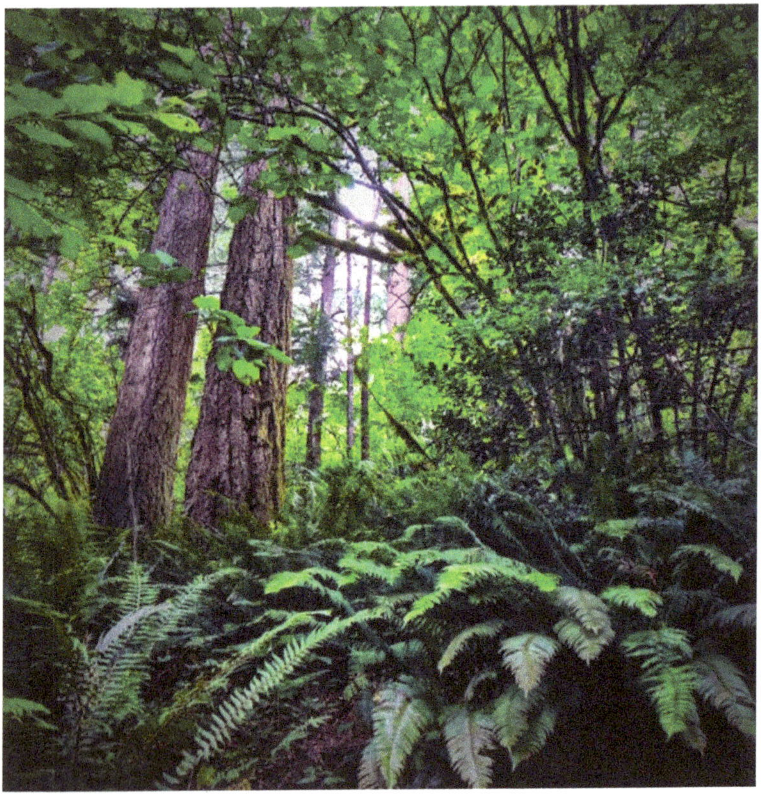

Sit by the creek and hear the birds tell you what's happening. Taking in an old growth forest is powerful. Be kind and careful, it's not ours.

Fresh Catch Recipes

Culinary Adventures

Found I had a passion early on and worked myself up into the high end restaurant & hospitality business in California. I posses the art. I was working as a Concierge in Lake Tahoe California when I Met Wolfgang Puck. Lake Tahoe Concierge Society scheduled a tour in San Francisco. The Concierge Society was powerful, we could bring your restaurant, a steady stream of top shelf clients. The Limousine picked us up at the swanky San Francisco Hotel and drove us to the "It," Restaurant. The highly trained restaurant staff was on point, they were experts in the craft. They wined and dined our exclusive club of elite advisors to impress. We toured seven exclusive restaurants. A different unforgettable course at every stop. Absolutely fantastic. I'll never forget it!

Old growth deep forests harvest some of the world's best kept culinary secrets. Salmon, chanterelle mushrooms, grapes and truffles are in high demand as Pacific Northwest seasonal delicacies. Deep in the woods you meet the real pickers. They are secretive and make a living doing it. Keep in mind, you have to know the owners that own the spots. Mushroom pickers are exclusive and often reclusive. They are not known to share their secrets. Chanterelles and truffels hold a high demand and higher price. Don't get me started on the Wineries and Breweries!

"So you caught a fish...now what?" Let's start with my Favorite.

Cream Cheese & Spinich Salmon

Ingredients & Directions

A personal favorite, bake or grill this masterpiece. Prepare and clean salmon. On heavy duty foil. Stuff the salmon with a cube of cream cheese. Add fresh spinach, chopped onions, dill, salt and pepper to taste. Bake for about an hour. Fish size will vary your cooking time. Serve with a fresh vegetable or side dish of your choice. Great for camping. Other versions substitute mayonnaise for your sauce. Be creative.

Ginger Honey Salmon

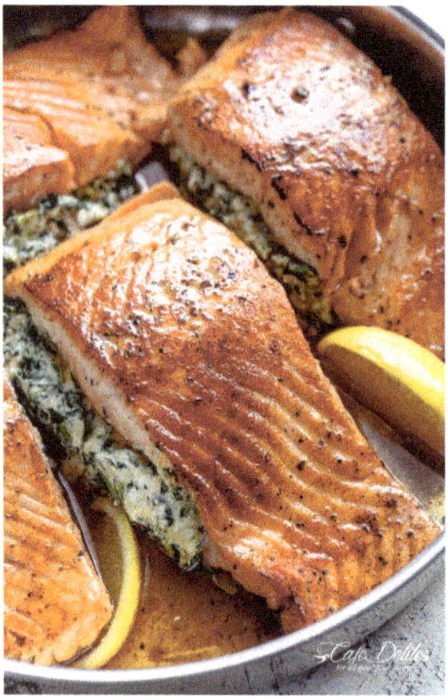

Chef's have a way of making food look fantastic. Mine did not quite turn out like this picture. However was absolutely delicious.

- 1/3 cup orange juice
- 1/3 cup reduced-sodium soy sauce
- 1/4 cup honey
- 1 green onion, chopped
- 1 teaspoon ground ginger
- 1 teaspoon garlic powder
- 1 salmon fillet (1-1/2 pounds and 3/4 inch thick)

Directions

- For marinade, mix first six ingredients. In a shallow bowl, combine salmon and 2/3 cup marinade; refrigerate 30 minutes, turning occasionally. Reserve remaining marinade for basting.
- Place salmon on an oiled grill rack over medium heat, skin side down; discard marinade remaining in bowl. Grill salmon, covered, until fish just begins to flake easily with a fork, 15-18 minutes, basting with reserved marinade during the last 5 minutes.

Health Tip: Everyone thinks of omega-3's when it comes to salmon, but it's also a good source of most B vitamins, which are important in energy production.

Source: tasteofhome.com

Provencal Salmon (Wolfgang Puck) Recipe

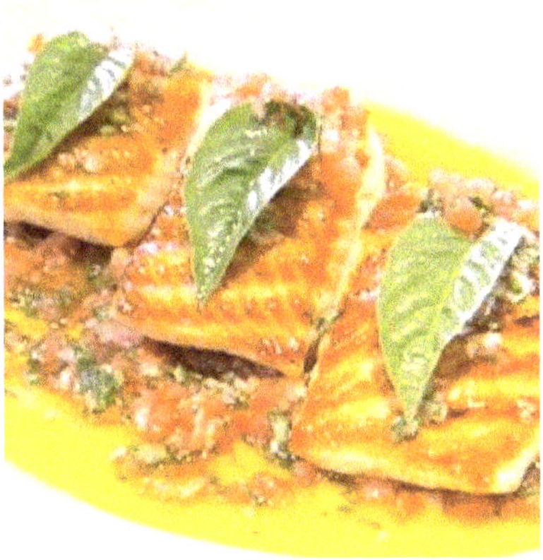

Ingredients

1 cup olive oil

2 tbsp sherry wine vinegar

1 bunch basil leaves, chopped

3 shallots, minced

4 ripe tomatoes, peeled, seeded, and chopped fine

1/2 lemon , zested and grated

1 tbsp minced fresh chives

1 tbsp minced fresh tarragon

salt , freshly ground pepper

2 carrots, peeled

1 leek, white part only

2 stalks celery , with strings removed

2 quarts court bouillon, recipe follows

2 lb chinook or king salmon fillets

2 medium carrots

2 stalks celery

1 leek

1 sprig fresh thyme

1 bay leaf

1 tsp salt

1/2 tsp freshly ground pepper

2 quarts water

Directions

1. Sauce Pistou:
2. Combine the olive oil, sherry vinegar, basil, shallots, tomatoes, lemon rind, chives, and tarragon. Season with salt and pepper to taste. Let marinate overnight, unrefrigerated.
3. Cut carrots, leek and celery into julienne. Cook them in 1 cup strained court bouillon until tender but still crisp. Drain and reserve.
4. Wrap each salmon fillet in foil and poach in court bouillon for approximately 5 minutes. To check the degree of doneness, remove 1 package from the liquid and unwrap. The center should still be slightly pink. To serve, divide julienne of vegetables among serving plates. Arrange salmon fillets in the center of the julienne and top each fillet with a tablespoon of the sauce pistou. Serve remaining sauce separately.
5. Court Bouillon:
6. Slice carrots, celery and leek into 1/4 inch pieces. Place in the bottom of a saucepan.
7. Add the remaining ingredients and bring to a boil. Boil for 20 minutes.
8. Yield: Makes about 2 quarts

Baked Salmon with Cucumber and Dill

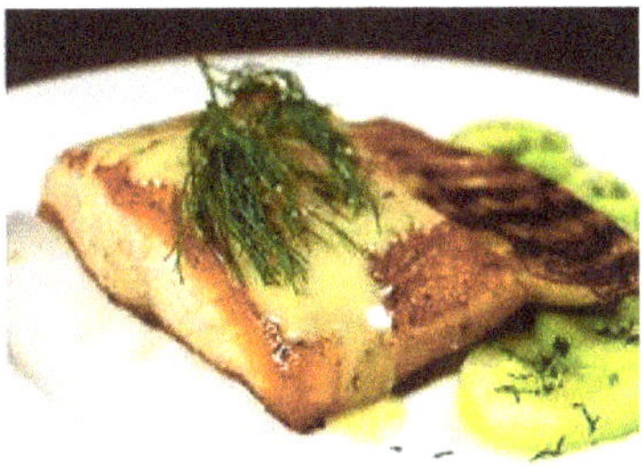

Ingredients

- 1 pound salmon fillets
- ¼ cup butter, melted
- 5 tablespoons lemon juice
- 1 tablespoon dried dill weed
- ¼ teaspoon garlic powder
- sea salt to taste
- freshly ground black pepper to taste
- cucumber at presentation

Directions

Instructions Checklist

- Step 1

Preheat oven to 350 degrees F (175 degrees C). Lightly grease a medium baking dish.

- Step 2

Place salmon in the baking dish. Mix the butter and lemon juice in a small bowl, and drizzle over the salmon. Season with dill, garlic powder, sea salt, and pepper.

- Step 3

Bake 25 minutes in the preheated oven, or until salmon is easily flaked with a fork.

Cucumber cold for final touch.

Pacific Northwest Smokehouse Goodness

The Pacific Northwest is known for our famous Smoked Salmon. Like our blackberries, mushrooms and tulips, it is a seasonal item in high demand. Dad built Grandpa a smokehouse and then built one for us. The yearly batch is so delicious. It is often gifted during holidays. The best culinary secrets are deep in the forest. Generations of brine formulas have been closely guarded. Like Whiskey, we will even give you the recipe. As every great Chef knows, it is in the detailed methods, an absolute art to the level of science. Every time I see a an old smokehouse I think of my Grandpa Jack. A tradition worth passing down. It's an art, like wine or brewing beer. Some smokers are well known for their product and it is in high demand around the holidays. Just like Hollywood, it's who you know.

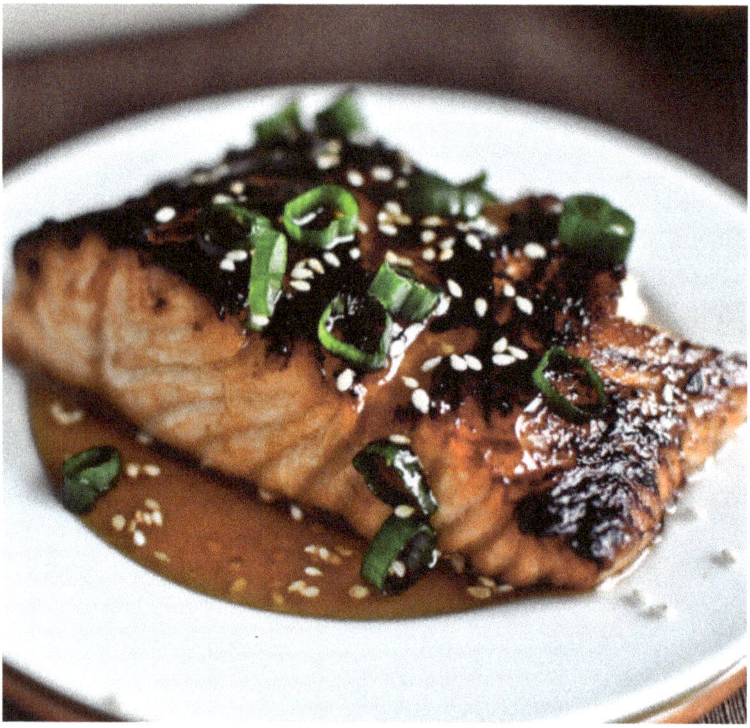

Casual or gourmet, Pacific Northwest Salmon has been a delicacy of humans since the beginning of humans. Little touches are a chef's secret. Presentation is crucial in the cutthroat restaurant business. What's gourmet here. The added shallots and sesame seeds. Take it over the top and impress your guests with gourmet touches.

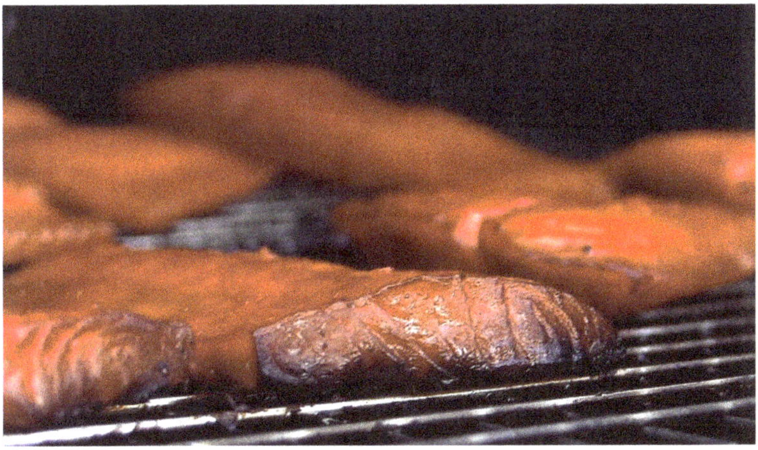

Pacific Northwest is known for the delicacy of Smoked Salmon. youtube.com

Jack & Dan's Smoked Salmon Brine

My Grandpa Jack new how to smoke top grade premium gourmet quality smoked salmon. Local guarded secret for generations.

1 Cup Sugar

1 Cup Water

1 Cup salt

1 Cup Brown Sugar

Brother Dan wrote: “It's all in the smoking. Alder chips work best. Grampa's secret was he would also sprinkle in a bit of green vine maple periodically during the entire smoking process. Smoke to your liking.” Darold's Dad, another Jack, used the same recipe substituting apple juice for the water. The mountain secrets have been revealed. Certain tastes and smell just speak to your family traditions. We are so blessed to live in the Pacific Northwest. I had to move away and come back to appreciate it.

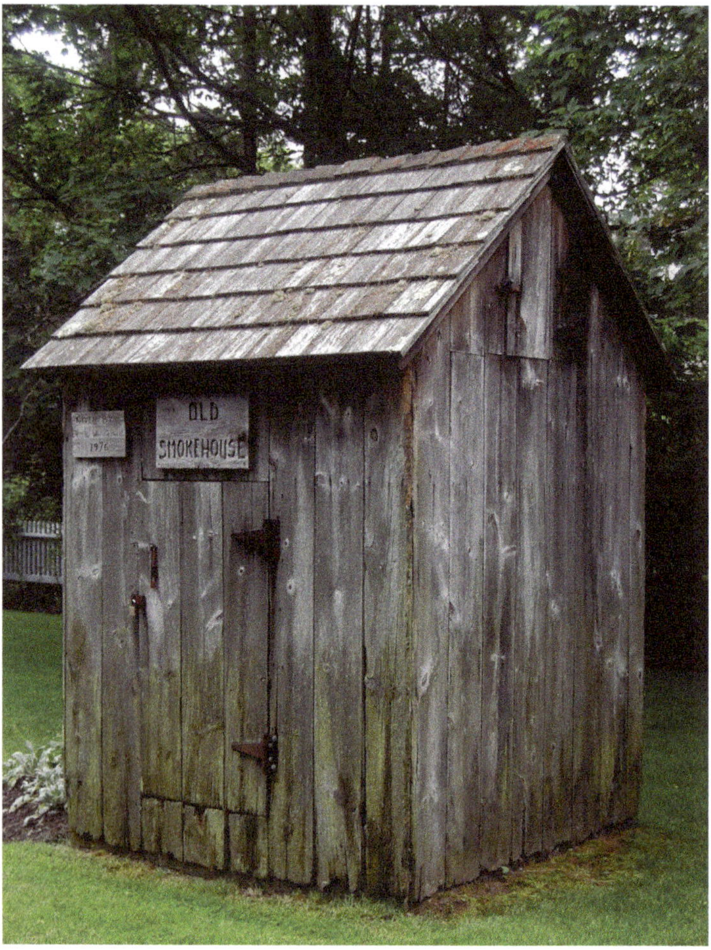

Every time I see a an old smokehouse I think of my Grandpa Jack. A tradition worth passing down. It's an art, like wine, making cheese or brewing beer.

#1 Best Brine Recipe of 2020

- maple syrup
- salt
- pepper
- 1 quart cold water
- 1 cup brown sugar

- 1/4 cup soy sauce
- 1 tablespoon black pepper
- yummly.com

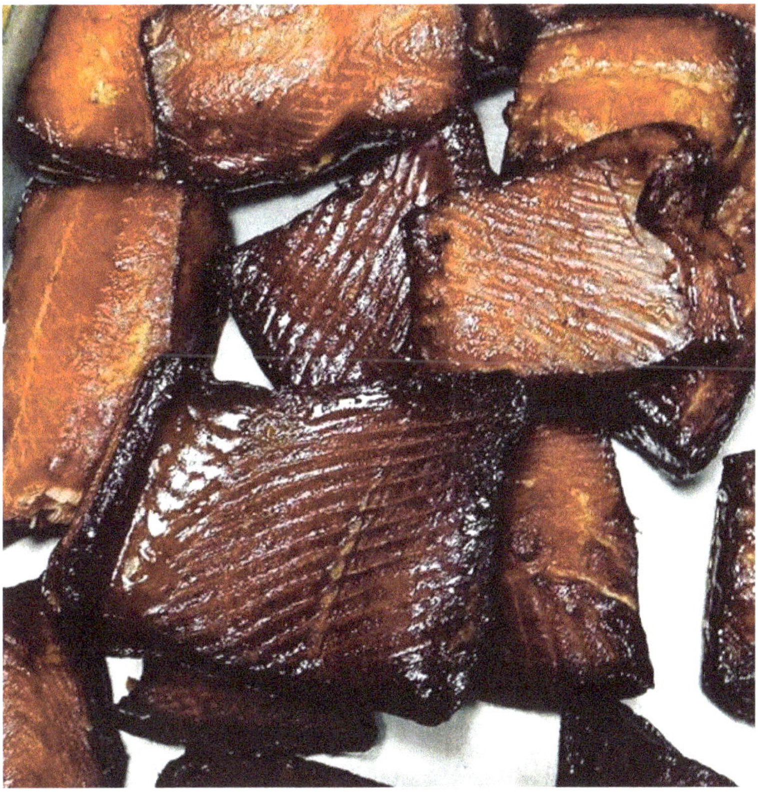

Authentic Pacific Northwest Smoked Salmon. A Pacific Northwest delicacy.

Maple and Brown Sugar Smoked Salmon

You won't believe how easy and delicious this Maple and Brown Sugar Smoked Salmon is! It's ready in less than 2-4 hours with just six simple ingredients and your smoker!

Brine 8-10 hrs Prep Time:20 min Cook Time 3-4 Hours

Ingredients:

- 2-3 LB Salmon
- Brine (recipe below)
- Maple syrup
- Salt and Pepper to taste

Brine: Combine and stir:

- 1 Quart cold water
- 1 Cup brown sugar
- ¼ Cup soy sauce
- 1 Tablespoon black pepper

Preperation

1. Clean the fish well and remove all of the small pin bones. These can sometime be tough to remove, so we recommend tweezers to grab them and pull out at an angle.
2. Place the salmon filet(s) into a resealable bag and cover with the brine. Place the bag into a
shallow dish or pan and set in the refrigerator for 8-10 hours.
3. Remove from the brine and pat dry with a paper towel to prevent the white fatty protein from oozing out during the smoke.
4. Start your grill and set temp to Smoke, or as low as it will go. When up to temp, place the salmon skin side down on the grill grates.
5. Smoke for about 2.5 hours.
6. At the 2.5 hour mark, lightly brush the salmon every 30 minutes until the salmon temp reaches 145-degrees
7. Remove from the grill and enjoy immediately, or allow to cool and enjoy whenever. bearmountainbbq.com

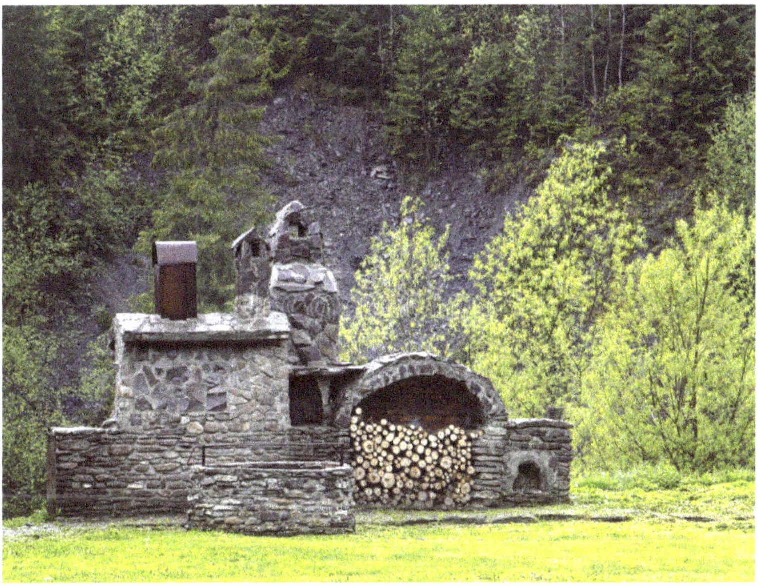

I found this great picture of an old smoke house on google images.

Deschutes River

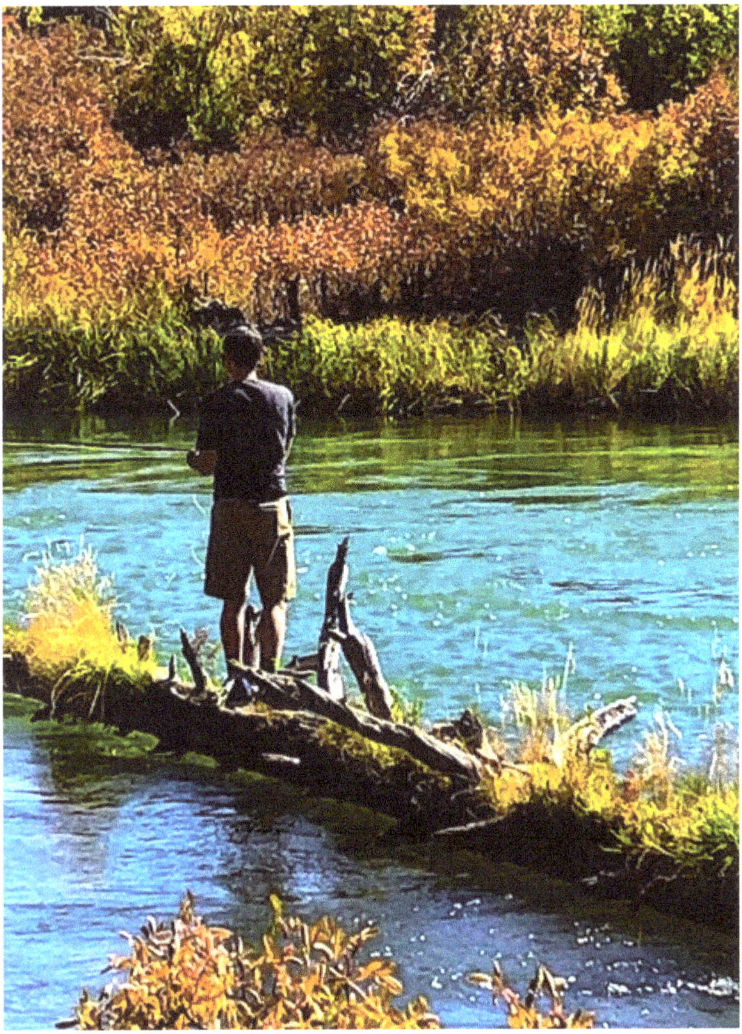

Darold fishing the Deschutes River in Oregon State.

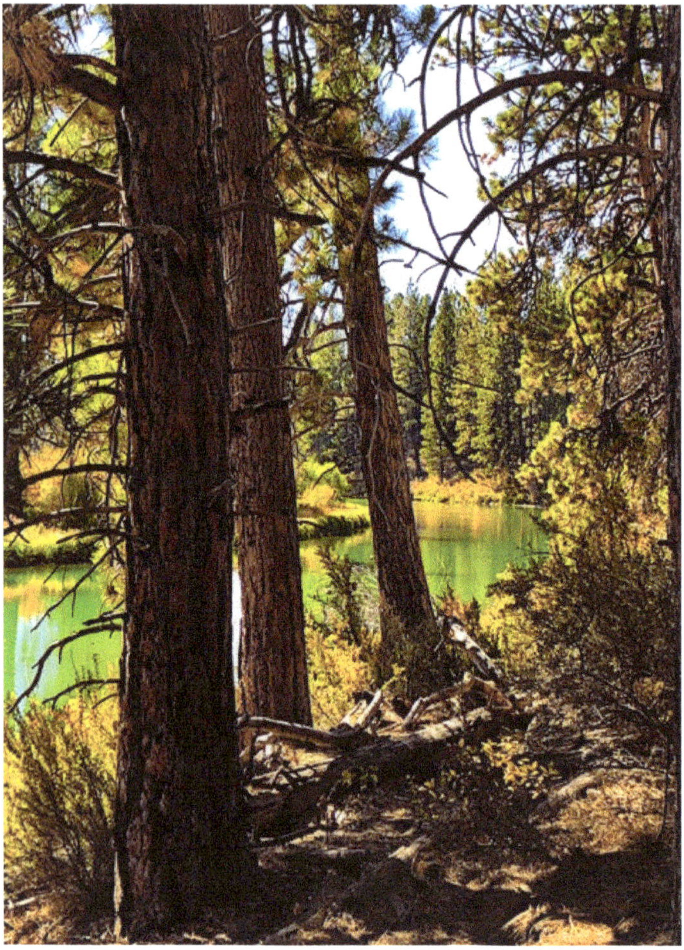

Underbrush is different East of the Mountains.

Bend Oregon

We took a weekend and went, "East of the Mountains," as locals call it. Oregon State hides a recreational playground. Deschutes River and the Bend Area is known as the best fly fishing and snow skiing in the world. Darold put his pole in for a few casts while I took photographs. Buddy Love sniffed and ran around the trails. We enjoyed the sunshine and explored the area.

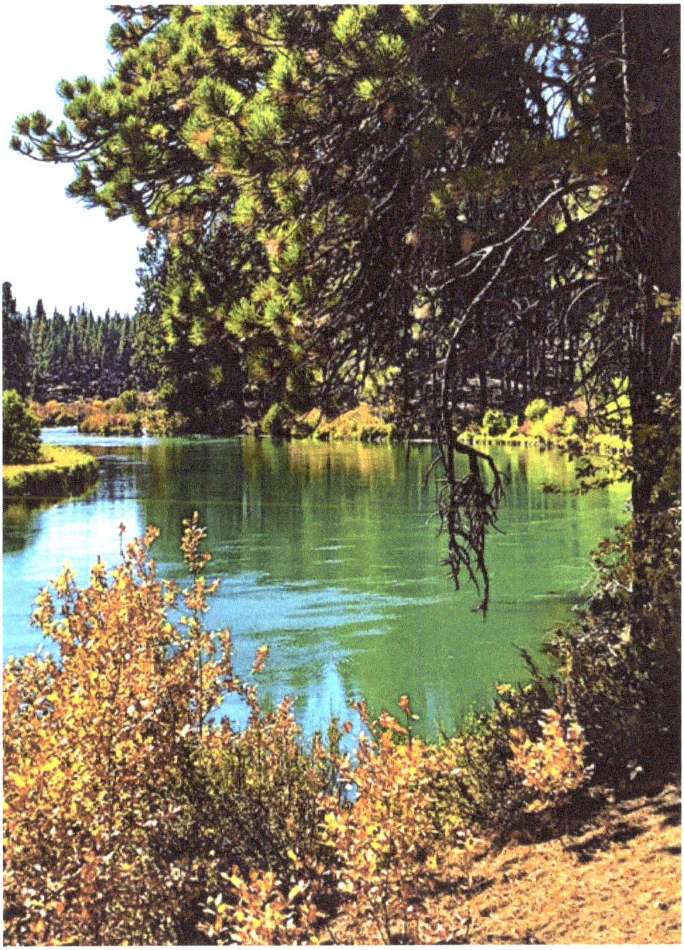

Deshutes River is a beautiful Fishing Experience.

The Deschutes River in central Oregon is a major tributary of the Columbia River. The river provides much of the drainage on the eastern side of the Cascade Range in Oregon, gathering many of the tributaries that descend from the drier, eastern flank of the mountains

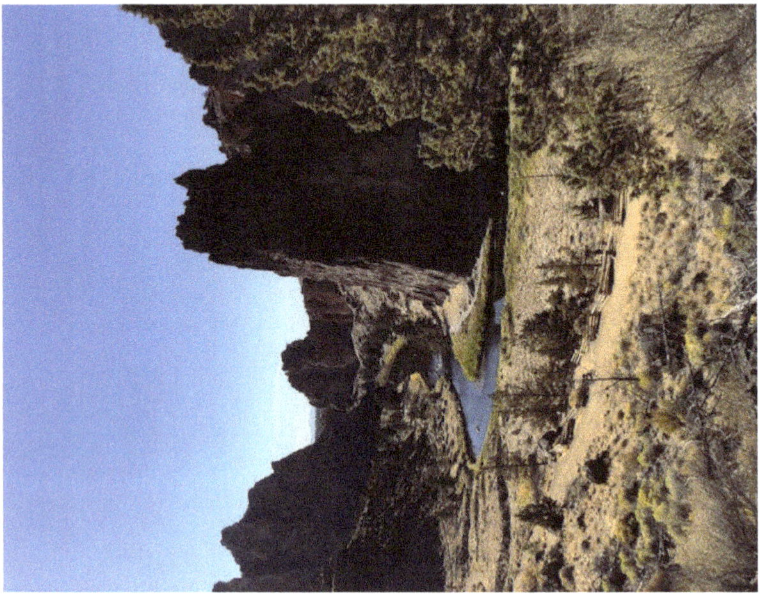

History staring right back at you.

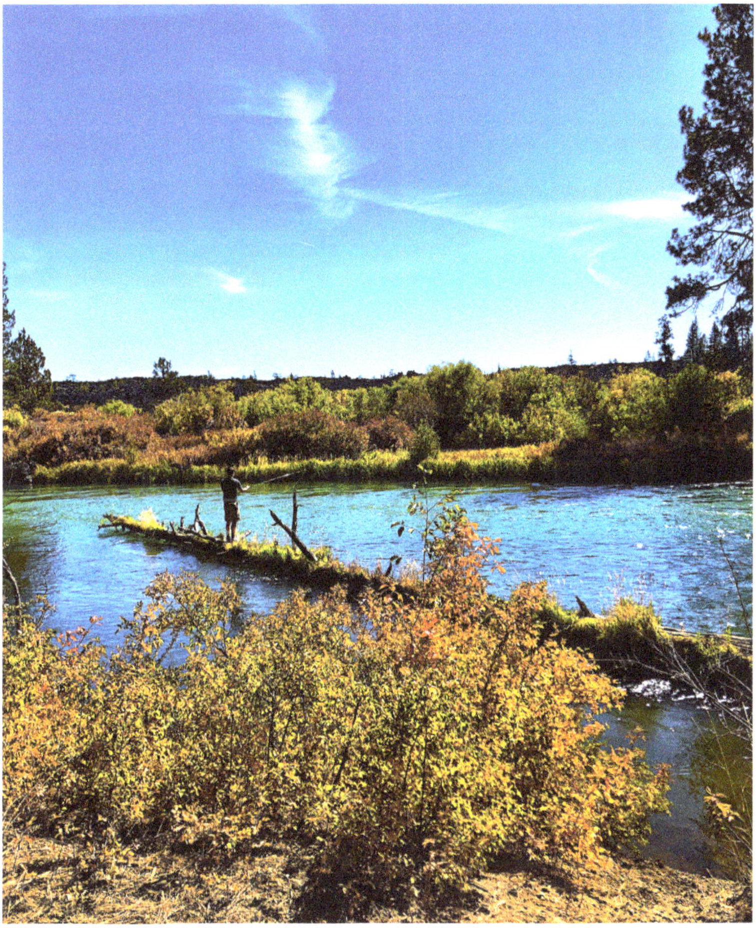

Great Day for Fishing the Deschutes River.

The Deschutes provided an important route to and from the Columbia for Native Americans for thousands of years, and then in the 19th century for pioneers on the Oregon Trail. The river flows mostly through rugged and arid country, and its valley provides a cultural heart for central Oregon. Today the river supplies water for irrigation and is ...

Mouth: Columbia River

Length: 252 mi (406 km)

Source: Little Lava Lake

State: Oregon

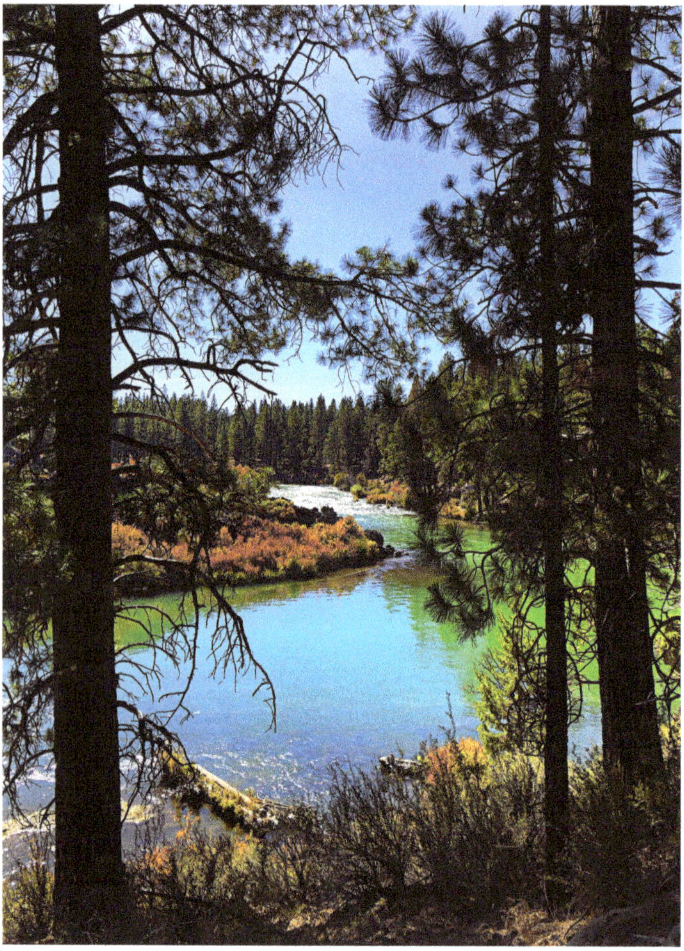

Quiet and peaceful Deschutes River, Oregon State

Deschutes River The **Deschutes River** is located in central Oregon. It provides much of the drainage on the eastern side of the Cascade Range on its way to its confluence with the Columbia River. The Deschutes was an important resource for thousands of years for Native Americans and in the 19th century for pioneers on the Oregon Trail.

Lake Mayfield

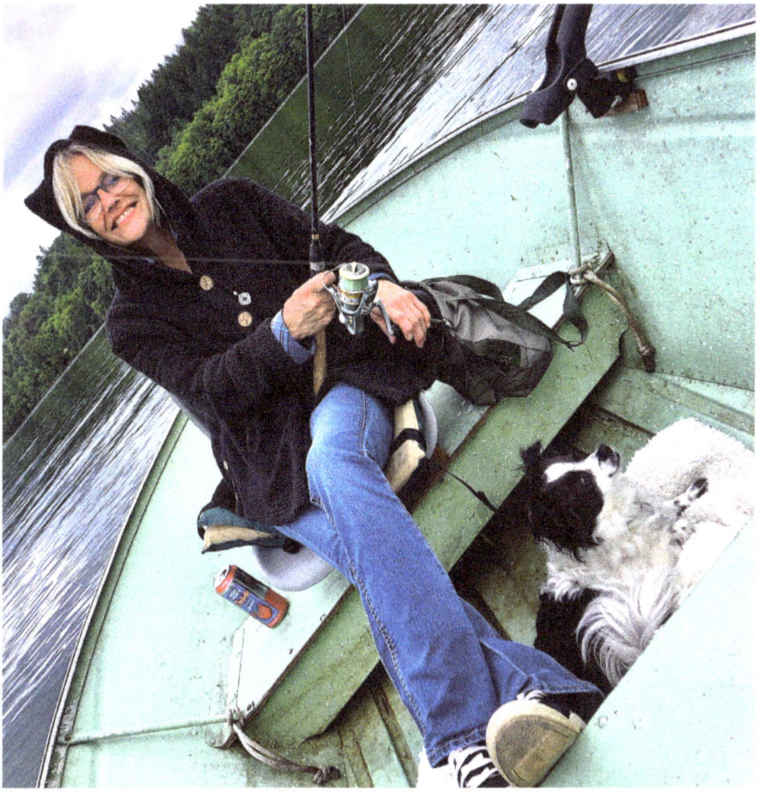

Distancing was not a new thing to me. I've played out in the woods my whole life.

This reservoir was formed by the construction of Mayfield Dam. It is managed for catchable rainbow trout and warmwater species. Tiger muskies were introduced in 1993 to help in controlling nuisance northern pikeminnow (squawfish) populations.

The lake is located about three miles west of Mossyrock. The big attraction is tiger musky fishing. The state record is currently over 31 pounds; larger ones are out there. The best tiger musky fishing is during the warmer months. Consult the current Sport Fishing Rules pamphlet for specific regulations at this lake.

Surplus hatchery Coho and fall Chinook may be placed in the lake for additional fishing opportunity. Yellow perch are also caught in fair numbers, and a few large mouth bass are present. Boating access is available at a Lewis County park just off of Highway US-12, at Ike Kinswa State Park, and at a private resort. There is fair shore fishing access at the state park and at the Mossyrock Trout Hatchery. Call Tacoma Power's toll free fishing line at 888-502-8690.

Two-pole fishing **is NOT allowed Life Jacket is required for each passenger as well as one to throw. Always carry your fishing license, they check you. How do we know. Two Uniformed Officers came by our boat on state of the art jet skis and checked our pole count and fishing license**

Oddly, the government road signs say Mayfield Lake. So do the maps. Locals don't call it that. They call it Lake Mayfield. Shorline access is good and public access limited and don't forget sunscreen.

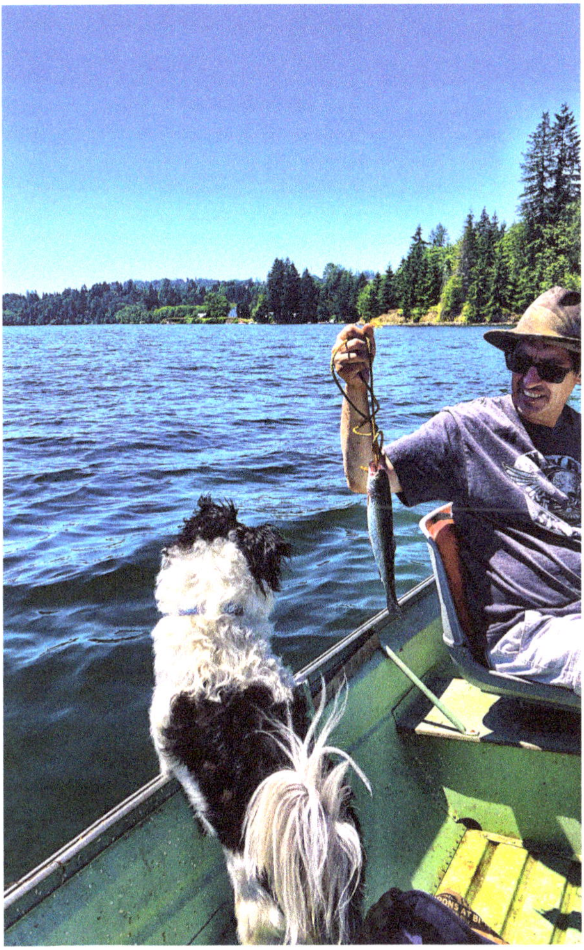

Darold and Buddy Love Fishing Lake Mayfield in Washington State

Species you might catch

- Brown bullhead
- Chinook salmon
- Coastal cutthroat trout (resident)
- Coho salmon
- Largemouth bass
- Northern pikeminnow

- Rainbow trout
- Tiger muskie
- Yellow perch

Lake information

County: Lewis
Acreage: 2021.90 ac.
Elevation: 428 ft.
Center: 46.545804, -122.530265

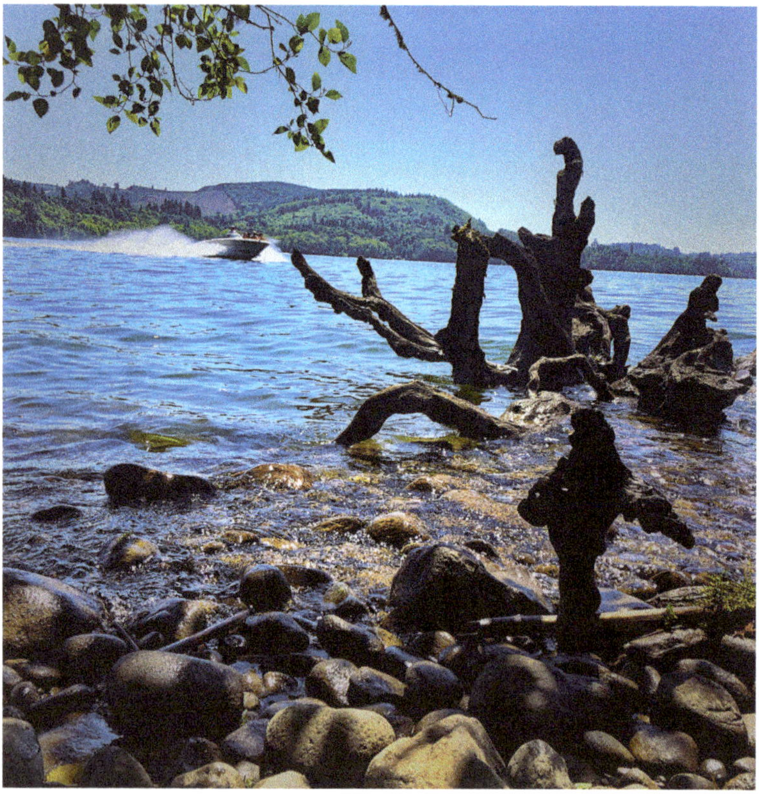

Boaters on Lake Mayfield having a great day. Nearby Riffe Lake is also a great fishing spot.

Ike Kinswa State Park

Ike Kinswa State Park is a great place to make summer memories. This classic state park sits on Mayfield Lake amidst a rolling patchwork of farmland 20 miles east of Interstate 5 and off U.S. Highway 12. Ike Kinswa provides idyllic days of boating, swimming and water sports for the whole family.

Fish for tiger muskie, largemouth bass, kokanee and rainbow trout; launch the family boat for water sports, or bring kayaks and paddleboards for a mellow float. Kids can splash in the swim area until the air turns cool, the daylight fades and the smell of barbecue draws them back to camp.

Campers can choose between quiet, forested tent and RV sites or lakeside cabins and snuggle in for the night after a busy day on the water.

Ike Kinswa State Park is a 421-acre camping park with 46,000 feet of freshwater shoreline on the north side of Mayfield Lake. In addition to its excellent boating, fishing and swimming options, the park offers short hiking trails, birding, wildlife viewing and two horseshoe pits.

Mayfield Resort and Marina

Recreation in Lake Mayfield is fantastic. Wake boarders dream. Campsites right on the water with access to your boat. Mayfield Resort & Marina is conveniently located on Lake Mayfield, and is your prime spot for Lake fun.Fishing, Boating, and relaxing lakeside. There is a Seasonal Restaurant on site, a convenient store open all year. Cabins, Lodging, RV parking, Tent camping, and much more. They are a family orientated business. RV Park and Campgrounds Source: Washington State Fish & Wildlife

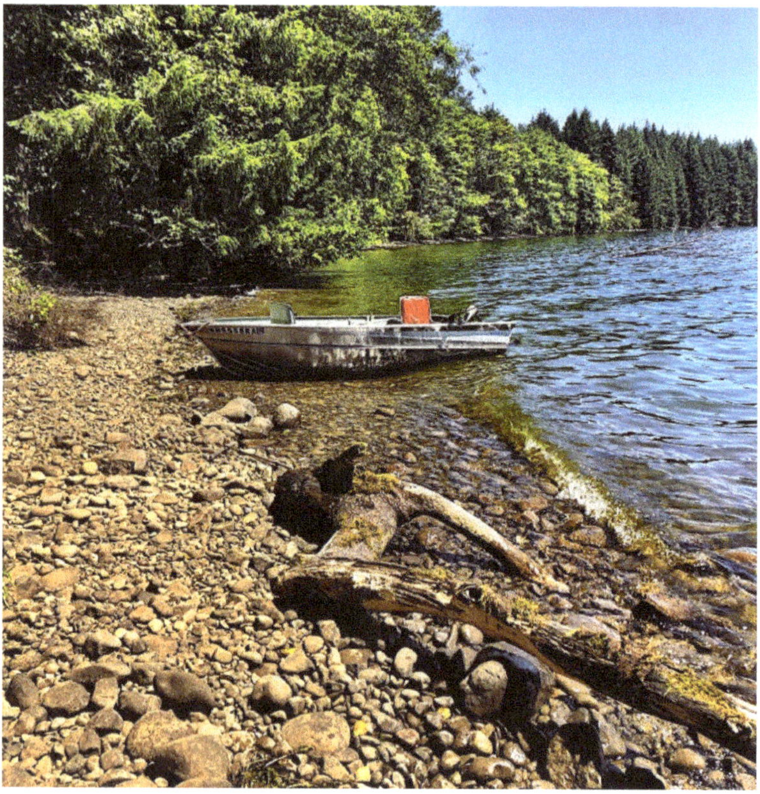

I found the most curious stick on this beach. It later landed in my Hat Shop UpriverStudios as The Wizard Stick! Movie set quality, it sold right away. UpriverStudios Link: etsy.me/3hGpVtv

The Old Fishing Boat

The boat had been sitting dormant a while. Filled with Family stories, rainwater and leaves. Darold gave it some love and fixed it up. Once again, she rides. We caught four Rainbow Trout and had an old fashioned picnic that day. Amid the wake-boarders and fancy boats, we landed some nice memories and fresh trout to take back to camp. Had some curious inquiries back at the boat launch. "Yes, there are fish in Lake Mayfield." It was obvious we were using the right set up. A known favorite, trolling a #3 Blue Spinner. The fly pole caught also caught two trout. The Old Fishing Boat was reborn that day.

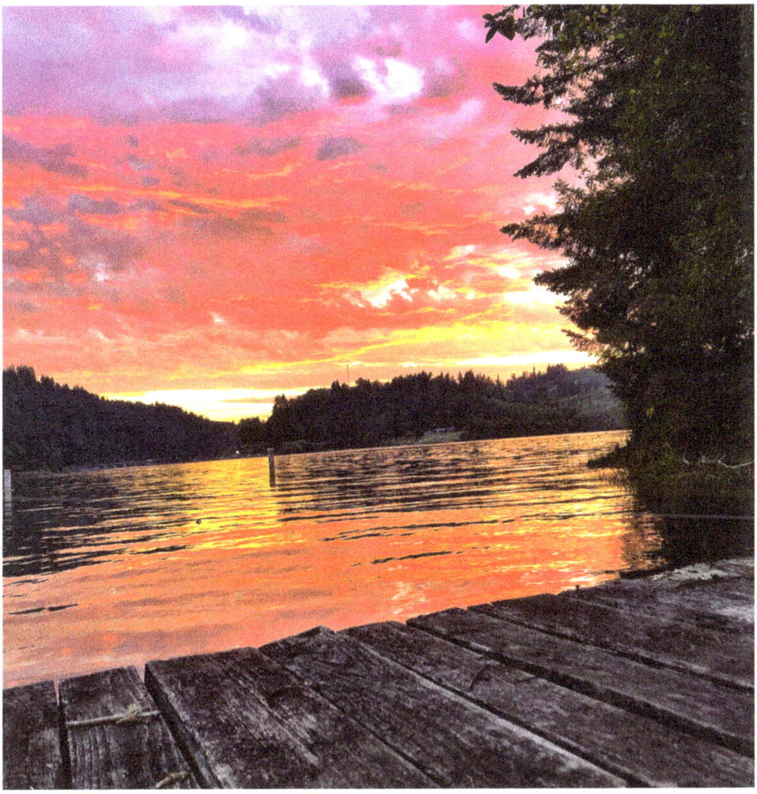

August Sunset on Lake Mayfield. Sunset shot from the dock.

Mayfield had quite a heyday in the 60s and 70s. All the jet-setters used to party here. It was a great way to show off your new boat, meet likewise friends and explore the beautiful Pacific Northwest. Located in the middle of Washington state, this overlooked playground has been a secret favorite of Washington locals and the surrounding area for generations. Going to Lake Mayfield for the weekend had clout, it was and still is, "cool." Many have treasured childhood memories at Lake Mayfield.

August, we picked blackberries for days, pollen rich and mountain sweet. The thorny bushes were loaded with fruit. We busted out the vintage iced cream maker and dessert was on the ready. Fresh catch trout to go with our steak dinner. The pacific northwest holds a lot of mysteries and a plethora of harvest. There are many books about Pacific Northwest mushrooms. True pickers make a seasonal living on forest harvests. Fantastic dinner.

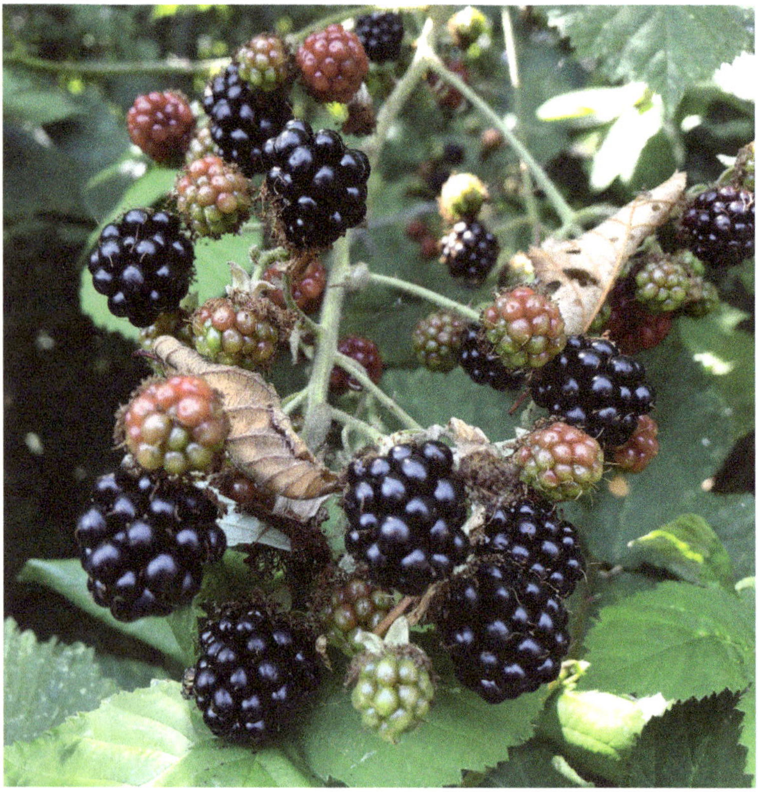

Homemade blackberry iced cream in the vintage iced cream maker was a special treat.

Swofford Pond

Swofford was originally designated to rear juvenile steelhead. When that proved to be unsuccessful, the focus turned towards managing the water for warmwater fish. There is a popular channel catfish and bass fishery that occurs on the pond as well.

This lake provides naturally reproducing populations of bluegill, crappie, largemouth bass, and brown bullheads.

Channel catfish have been stocked. Swofford also receives plants by Tacoma Power of several thousand catchable-size rainbow. There is an unimproved boat launching area. Internal combustion engines are not allowed. Call Tacoma Power's toll free fishing line at 888-502-8690.

Two-pole fishing **is allowed**

Shoreline access: Good

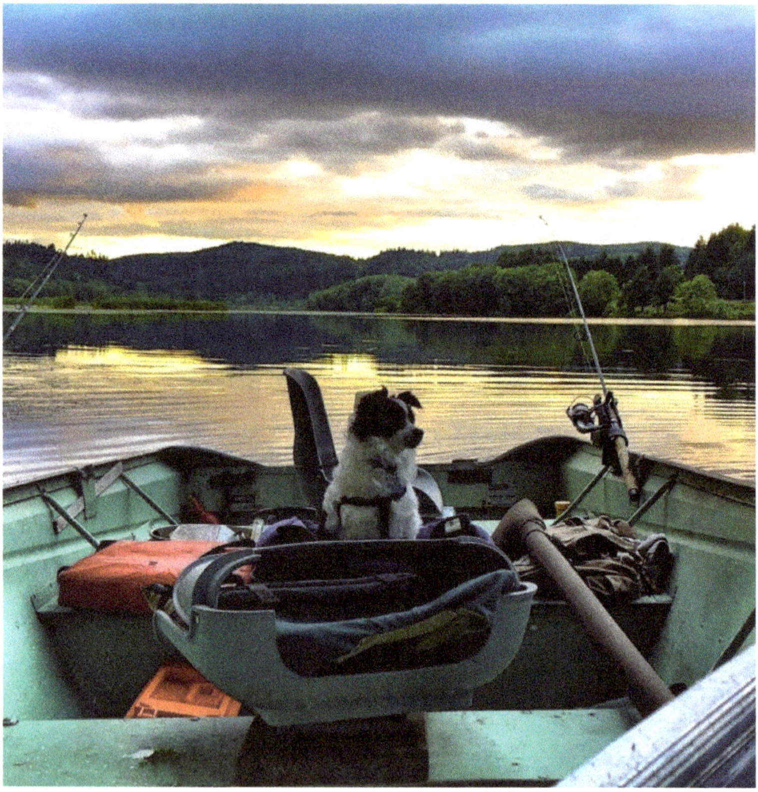

Buddy Love patiently waiting.

Species you might catch

- Brown bullhead
- Brown trout
- Channel catfish
- Pumpkinseed Sunfish
- Rainbow trout
- Smallmouth bass
- Warmouth
- Yellow perch

Lake information

County: Lewis
Acreage: 216.50 ac.
Elevation: 781 ft.
Center: 46.497908, -122.404393

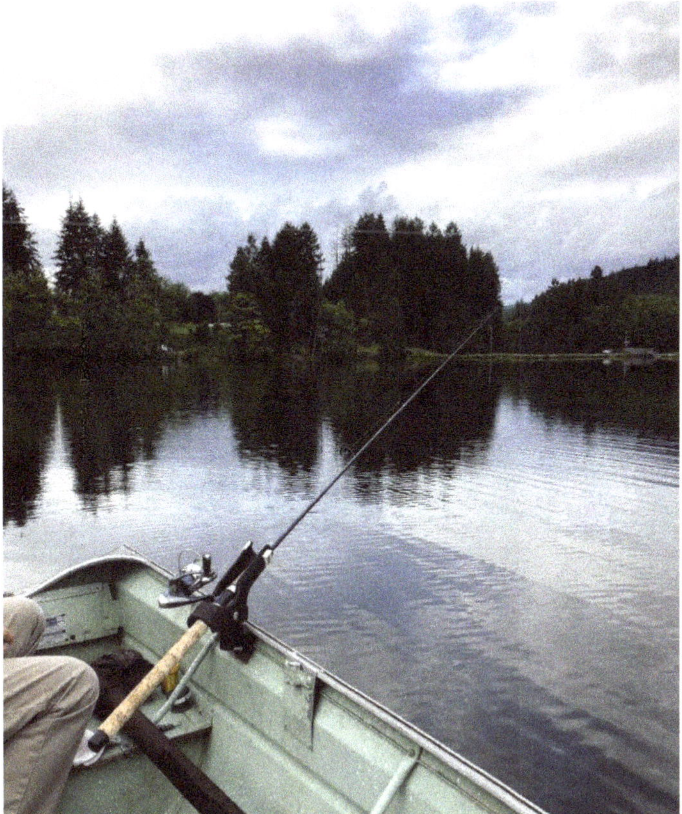

The Old Boat hits Swofford Pond for date night.

Sunset at Swofford Pond

The bank was lined with fisherman. It's a rugged boat launch. I wouldn't bring the yacht. Upon arrival we were immediately catching fish. This would be a great place to introduce a first timer. We caught seven fish. Crappies are perfectly edible. We did choose keep two Cutthroat Trout. We used blue spinners.

It was difficult to get photos as the fish were biting so often. We have friends who are kinfolk of the Swofford Family. The weather was perfect. Absolutely stunning. Ideal spot to teach and learn. Great date night.

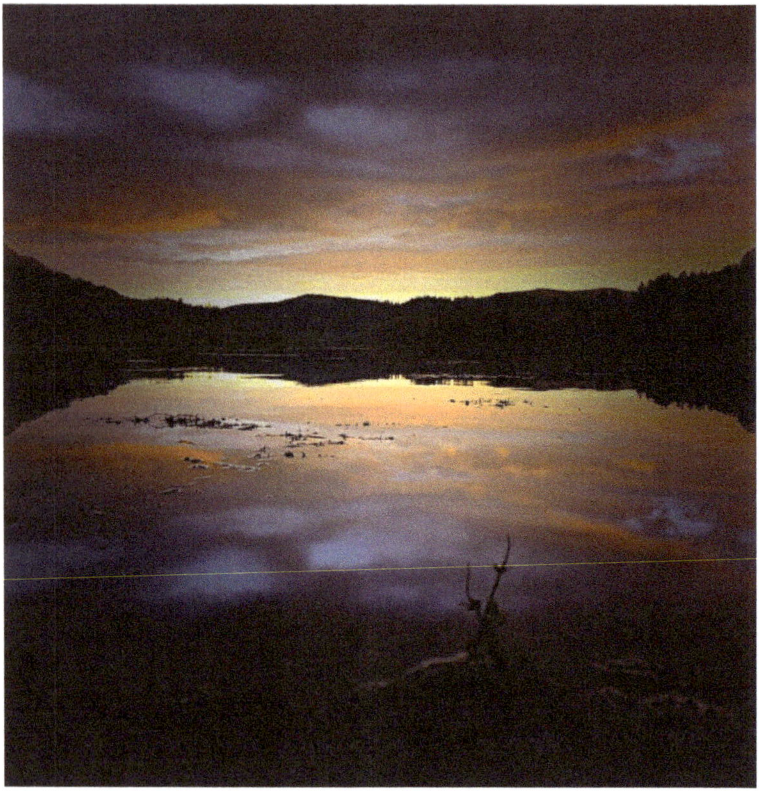

Sunset at Swofford Pond in the Beautiful Pacific Northwestl

Cowlitz River

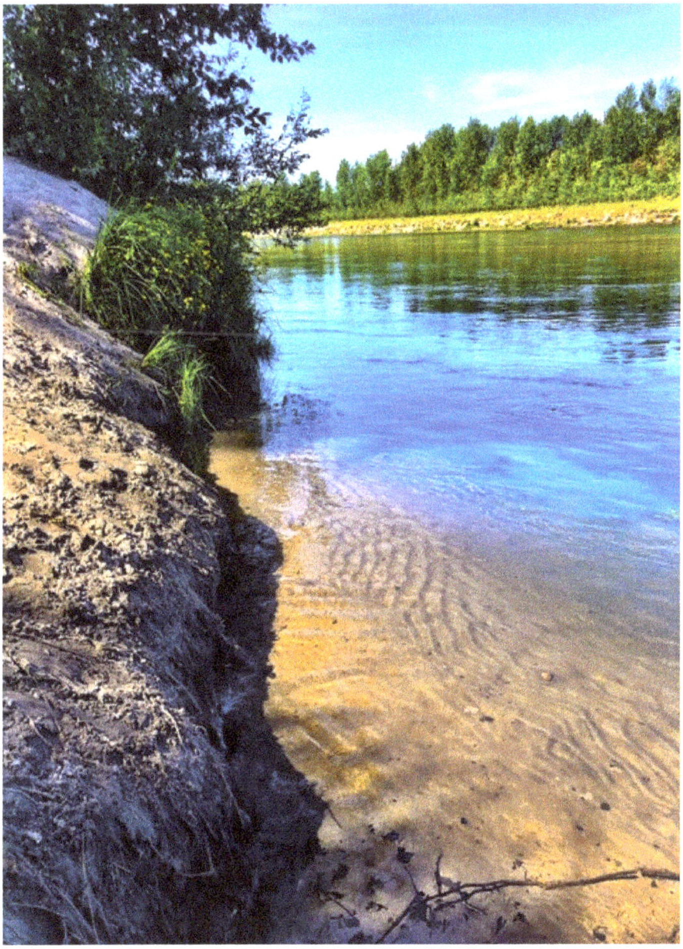

Cowlitz River at Castle Rock Washington. Volcanic ash from Mt. St. Helens line the riverbanks.

The **Cowlitz River** is a river in the state of Washington in the United States, a tributary of the Columbia River. Its tributaries drain a large region including the slopes of Mount Rainier, Mount Adams, and Mount St. Helens.

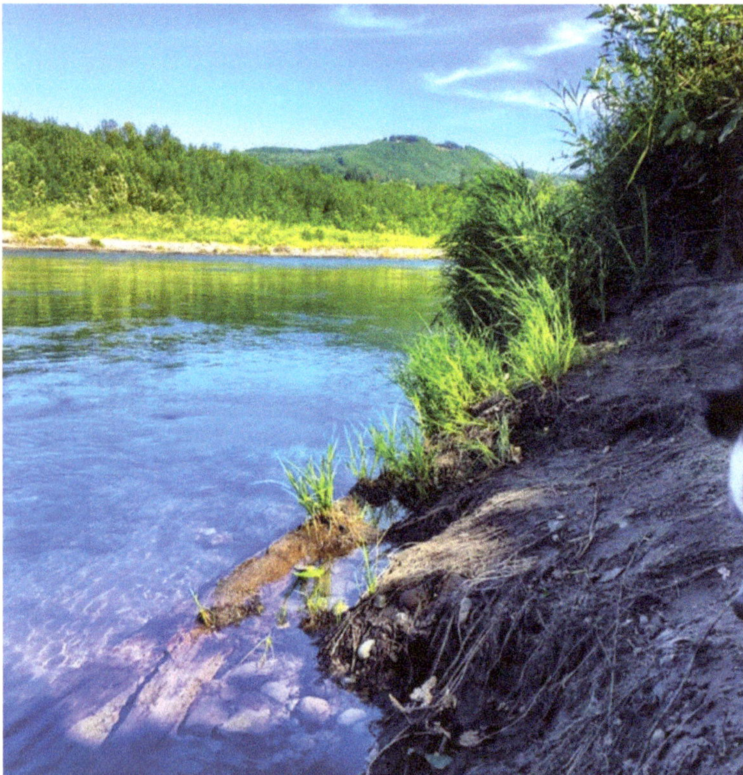

The water was clear. 1980 Mt. St. Helens destroyed this river. Yearly run of smelt brings thousands to the area for the annual tradition of smelt dipping. Most of us were born just a float downriver from this spot.

The Cowlitz has a 2,586-square-mile (6,698 km^2) drainage basin,[5][6] located between the Cascade Range in eastern Lewis County, Washington and the cities of Kelso and Longview. The river is roughly 105 miles (169 km) long, not counting tributaries.

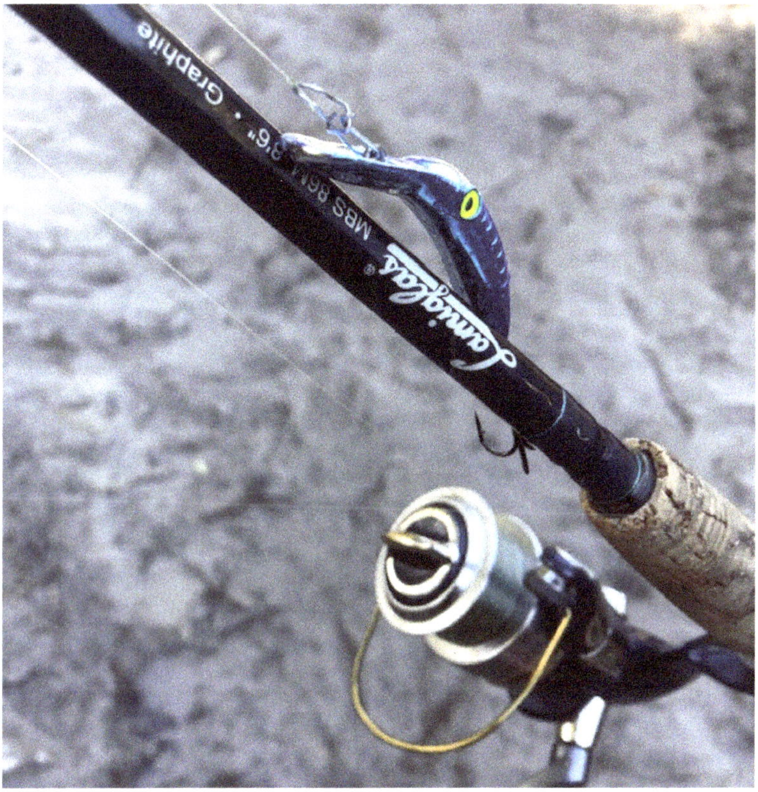

21 miles south Woodland Washington has two famous fishing outfits. Lamiglas and G.Loomis. Both are top grade with quality products. Longview WA has the locally known Bob's Merchandise & Sporting Goods est. 1947 by Bob Schlecht Sr. Fisherman's and Mill workers go-to. for quality products.

Major tributaries of the Cowlitz River include the Cispus River and the Toutle River, which was overtaken by volcanic mudflows (lahars) during the May 1980 eruption of Mount St. Helens.

When the smelt spawn in the Cowlitz River, the gulls go into a feeding frenzy that lasts for weeks. Kelso, Washington is known as the "Smelt Cap.

Cowlitz people

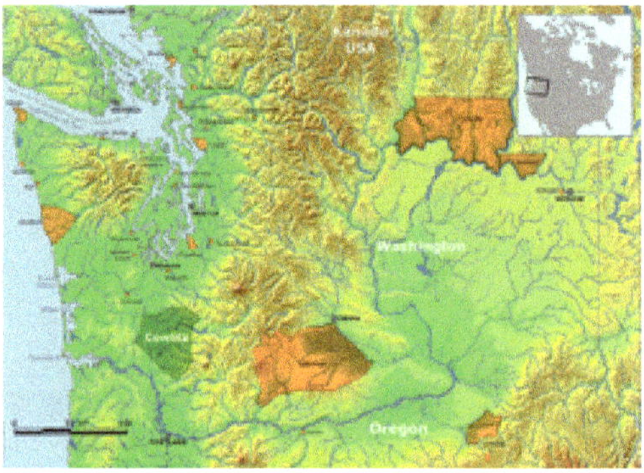

Traditional Cowlitz territory

Languages

English, Cowlitz, Sahaptin

Related ethnic groups

Chehalis, Quinault

The term **Cowlitz people** covers two culturally and linguistically distinct indigenous peoples of the Pacific Northwest. The **Lower Cowlitz** or **Cowlitz proper**, a southwestern Coast Salish people, which today are enrolled in the federally recognized tribes: Cowlitz Indian Tribe, Quinault Indian Nation, and Confederated Tribes of the Chehalis Reservation; and the **Upper Cowlitz / Cowlitz Klickitat** or **Taitnapam**, a Northwest Sahaptin speaking people, part of the Confederated Tribes and Bands of the Yakama Nation.

Their traditional homelands are in western Washington state in the United States.

Cowlitz tribal groups or bands

There is an ongoing dispute over the Cowlitz people, their history, territory, ancestry, ethnicity, and language; which is important for land claims and treaty negotiations with the U.S. government by Cowlitz descendants.

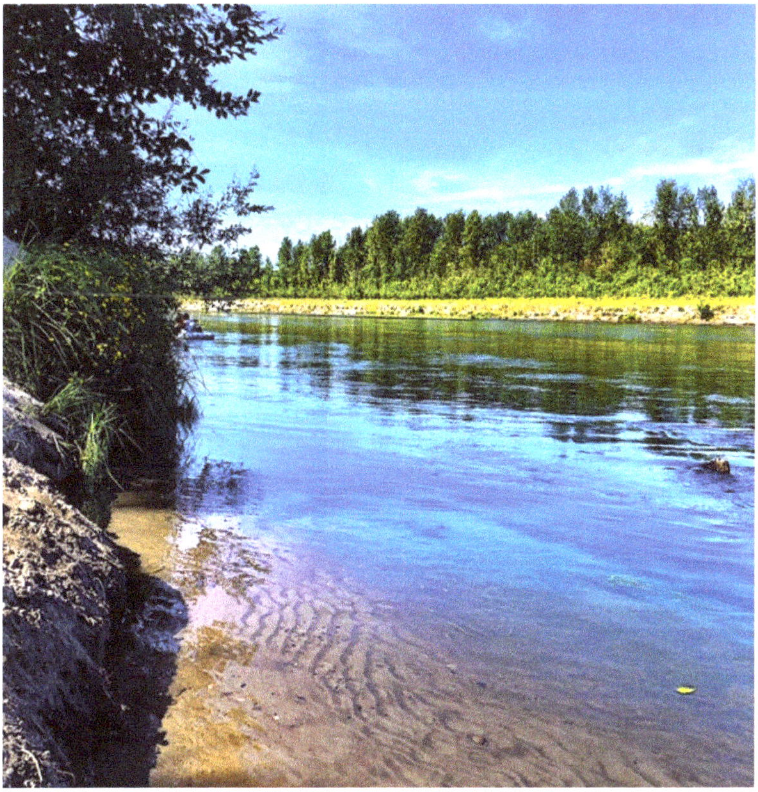

Cowlitz River is historically known for smelt dipping. Smoked smelt was a seasonal thing. Also used as bait for Salmon.

- the **Lower Cowlitz** or **Cowlitz proper** ("The People Who Seek Their Medicine Spirit", occupied 30 villages along the Lower Cowlitz River, other villages along the Toutle River; today the majority are enrolled within the Cowlitz Indian Tribe, some are part of Quinault Indian Nation, and Confederated Tribes of the Chehalis Reservation)

- the **Upper Cowlitz**, sometimes called **Stick Indians**, today identified as Sahaptin-speaking **Taidnapam** ("People of the Tieton River", occupied and controlled fourteen villages along the Upper Cowlitz River (shch'il) above Morton and Mossyrock, other villages along the Cispus River (shíshpash), and the Tilton River (laláIx) and had frequent contact with their Upper and Lower Yakama and Klickitat kin who lived on the east side of the Cascade Range and spoke Sahaptin. They apparently intermarried with Salish-speaking Lower Cowlitz communities downriver and travelled freely as far as the mouth of the Cowlitz River but were not originally Salish-speaking people. Their own name *Taitnapam* indicates that they originally came from east of the Cascades - along the Tieton River (in Yakama: Táitin) hence territory of the *Nahchísh-ƛlama*, a Yakama/Lower Yakama band along the Naches River and had strong linguistic and family ties to that band and to the Klikatat / Klickitat; today as *Yakima Cowlitz* or *Cowlitz Klickitat Band* part of the Confederated Tribes and Bands of the Yakama Nation).
- the **Lewis River Cowlitz**, sometimes called **Lewis River Chinook**, today considered to be regional group of **Taidnapam** (lived along Upper Lewis River and uppermost Nisqually River as neighbors to their Sahaptin kin the Mishalpam (Mical-ɬa'ma) ("Eatonville people", lit. "Mashel River people") and Klickitat; today as *Lewis River Klickitat Band* part of the Confederated Tribes and Bands of the Yakama Nation)
- the **Mountain Cowlitz** or **Kwalhiokwa Cowlitz** (lived between the Upper Chehalis River in the north and in the Willapa Hills to the south, intermarried with Salish-speaking Upper Chehalis (Kwaiailk) and the now extinct Northern Athapaskan-speaking Willapa (Kwalhioqua); today part of the Confederated Tribes of the Chehalis Reservation)
- Source: Wikpedia

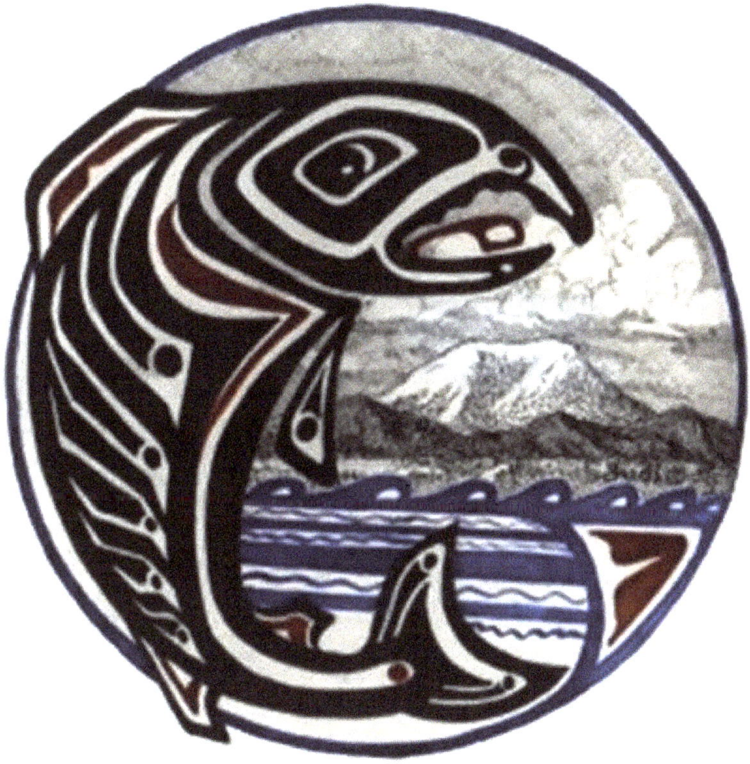

Image: thereflector.com

Kalama River

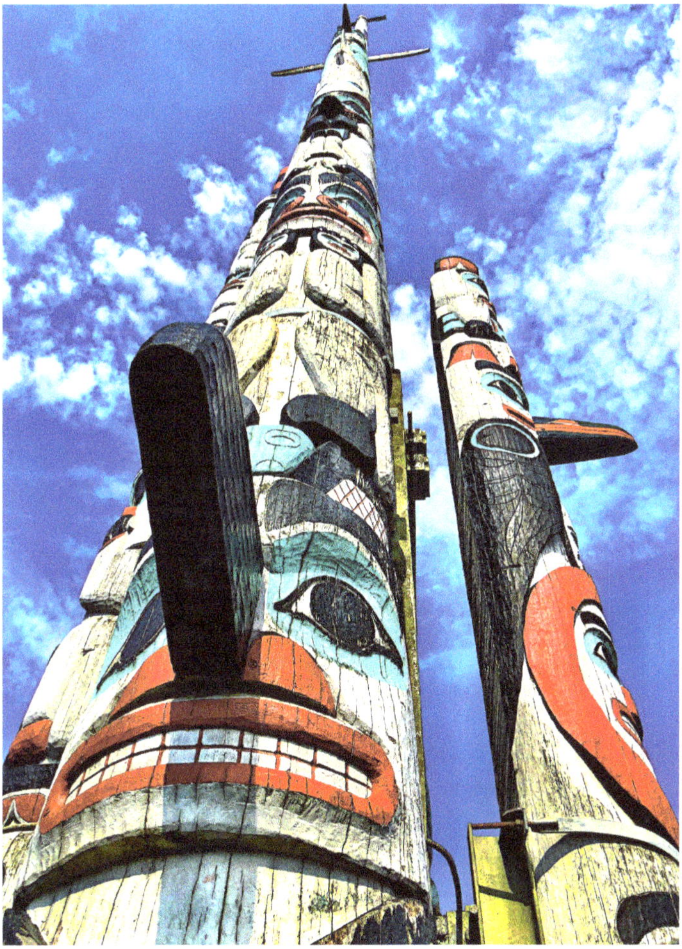

Tallest totems in the world. Lasoolka, local carver. These historic masterpeices are located at The Kalama Harbor Lodge. Go find the secret rooms. https://www.mcmenamins.com/kalama-harbor-lodge

Lelooska, Master Carver, Won Acclaim For His Totem Poles

ARIEL, Cowlitz County - Master carver and storyteller Lelooska, who dedicated much of his life to the preservation of the art and lore of Northwest Indians, has died.

He died of cancer Thursday. He was 63.

Lelooska was born Don Smith in Sonora, Calif. He was called Yana the Bear at birth, but it was the name Lelooska, meaning "To Cut Against Wood With a Knife," that brought him fame.

He came to Hubbard, Ore., in 1936 where his family ran a gift shop and where he carved for the tourist trade.

Lelooska won acclaim for his totem poles, carved out of old-growth cedar. He is said to have carved 100 or more totem poles and thousands of masks, using only the D adze, the elbow adze and the hooked knives used by his ancestors.

"My warrior grandfather was a whittler," Lelooska once told an interviewer. "He taught me to carve as soon as I could hold a knife."

Lelooska's grandfather, He-Kill, a full-blooded Cherokee, also taught him the myths and legends of his people.

"Grandfather always told me, `Let the hatchet be buried. But let not the Indian ways be forgotten.' "

During Oregon's Centennial in 1959, Lelooska carved a 50-foot totem pole celebrating the state's role in Operation Deep Freeze, which established a scientific station at the geographic South Pole. The pole now towers over Washington Park Zoo in Portland.

He carved a duplicate 30-foot Friendship pole, which dominates the entrance to the international airport at Christchurch, New Zealand.

In 1961, the family moved to Ariel. Volunteers built a traditional longhouse, a log museum and later an art gallery, where Lelooska and his family, wearing the masks and robes of the Kwakiutls, danced in the flickering shadows of the firelight.

Lelooska, with his pipe-organ voice, brought to life the myths and legends of his ancestors.

The longhouse shows were among his proudest accomplishments, attracting 25,000 visitors a year. There were also workshops in American Indian culture offered by the nonprofit Lelooska Foundation, where students can earn college credits from Central Washington University and Lewis & Clark College.

Lelooska received an honorary doctorate from Lewis & Clark for his leadership in American Indian art and culture. He also was given the school's Aubrey Watzek Award for his contributions to American Indian culture.

In 1968, Chief James Sewid, hereditary chief of the Kwakiutl Nation on Vancouver Island, held a potlatch to adopt Lelooska into the Sewid family.

Private services were planned at the Coast House at the family compound here.The **Kalama River** is a 45-mile (72 km) tributary of the Columbia **River**, in the U.S. state of Washington. It flows entirely within Cowlitz County, Washington. Calama **River** is an old variant name. Gabriel Franchere in 1811 wrote of the Indian village at the mouth of the **Kalama River**, adding that it was called Thlakalamah.

Kalama River begins on the southwest slope of Mount St. Helens and flows nearly 45 miles west-southwest and enters the Columbia River at River Mile (RM) 73, just downstream of the town of Kalama. The Lewis River is located 14 miles upstream and the Cowlitz River is located 7 miles downstream. Across from the mouth of the Kalama River on the Oregon shore was located the Trojan Nuclear Facility, and Prescott Beach, the location of Lewis and Clark's campsite of November 5, 1805. Seattle Times

Trojan Nuclear Plant

The Trojan Nuclear Facility was demolished May 11th 2006. It was somewhat of a celebrated local event with the cheers of many onlookers.

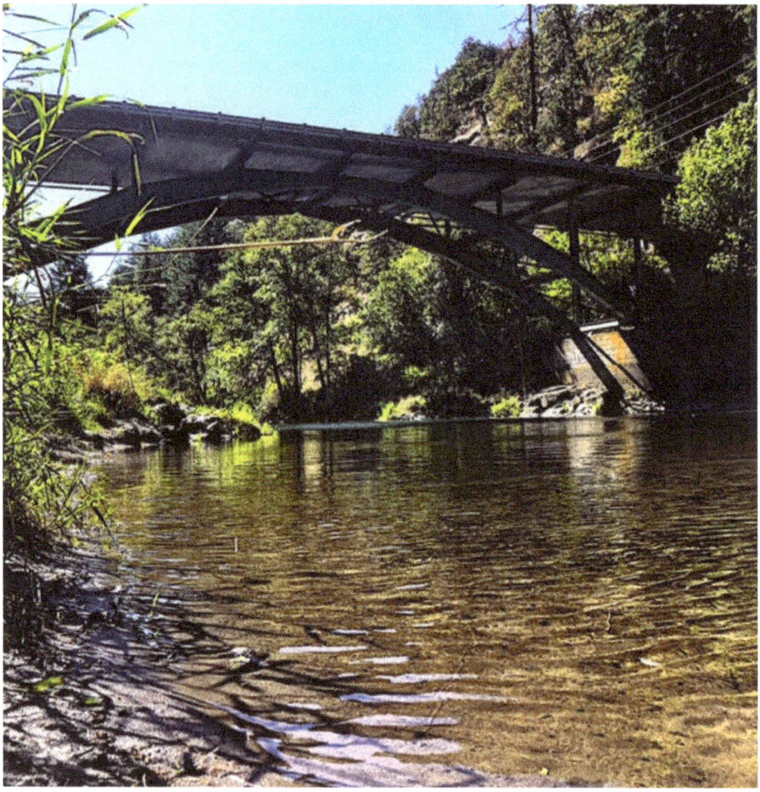

Yes, this is the bridge you can see fish. Truckers beware, she's a tight one.

Fishing the Kalama

Kalama is one of those, Best Kept Secret, places. They don't brag much about the fishing. They quietly keep it to themselves until the fish are running.

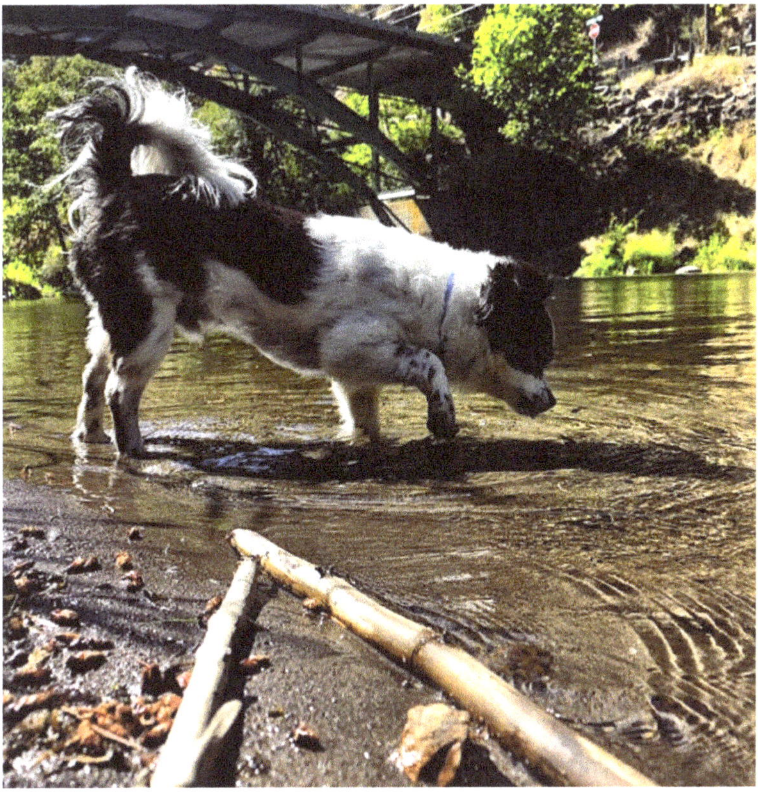

Buddy Love takes a dip. It was 98 degrees on our photo shoot day.

Take a Hike

Lake hike or river hike? How about a hike with both! Start with an exploration up the verdant Kalama River, then proceed to McBride Lake.

Begin at the Kalama Horse Camp trailhead and head east upstream along the river. At 0.2 mile, the trail descends slightly to cross a tributary on a small footbridge. Turn right to stay on the Toutle Trail and follow the river upstream. The route proceeds through the Cinnamon Trail junction and continues along the Kalama.

The river valley is lush and quiet, but you can tell it has a darker past. The dark black basalt along the water hints at the area's volcanic history. Today, however, the river's soft pools and mossy forests are hardly intimidating.

At 0.7 mile, the trail switchbacks to the top of a ridge with views of Mount St. Helens, Goat Mountain and Mount Adams. On bluebird days, you may even be lucky enough to get a peek at far-off Mount Hood.

The trail snakes back down to the water at 1.6 miles, and then crosses an old logging road at 2 miles. Continue on, climbing very slightly through mixed conifer forests with a decent spread of old-growth timber. Along the river, look for sneaky American
dippers flying in and out of the water. At 3.3 miles, turn right on an abandoned road, the Blue Horse Trail, and cross the Kalama.

On the other side, turn left to follow the Toutle Trail past a small waterfall and McBride Lake's south shore. This meadowy river valley occasionally hosts grazing Roosevelt elk, as well as a happy collection of birds and small forest critters. The trail then climbs away from the lake, but this makes a good place to enjoy lunch before heading back by the same route.

WTA Pro Tip: This trail winds in and out of the Mount St. Helens National Volcanic Monument, so be sure to observe all posted signage, including pet restrictions.

Source: WTA.org

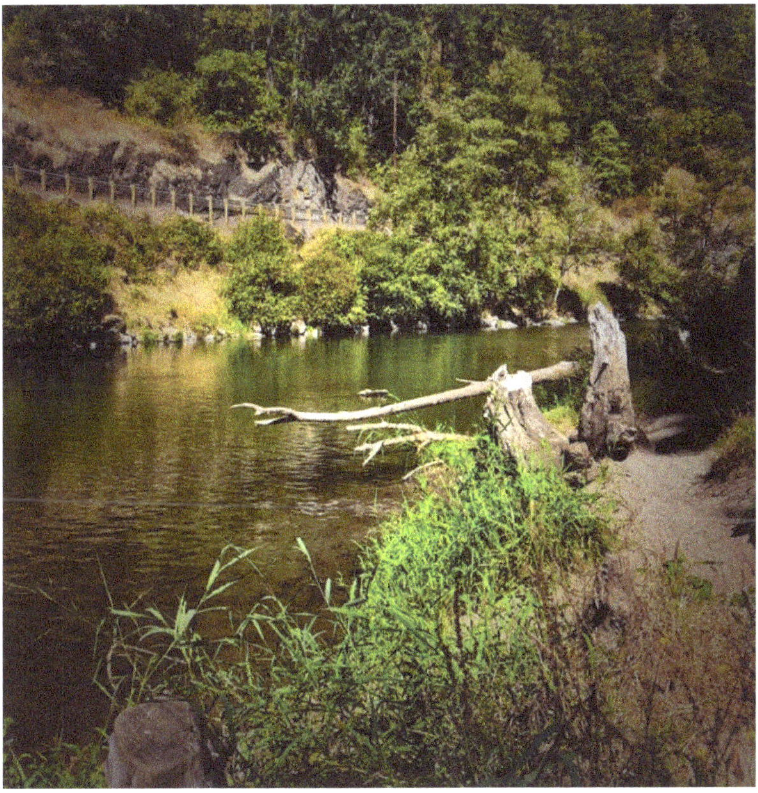

Rich in history, the river has provided for many generations.

Kalama History

Kalama, Washington (the City)

The town of Kalama, Washington, is located at Columbia River Mile (RM) 75, and lies just upstream of the mouth of the Kalama River. Kalama was built by the Northern Pacific Railroad in 1870 during the construction of a rail line from Tacoma, Washington, to Portland, Oregon.

The Name

The name "Kalama" is an Indian name meaning "beautiful", "stone", or "pretty maiden". The name "Kalama" was first mentioned in 1806 in the Lewis and Clark Journals ("Cath la haws Creek", "Calams River", and "Calamas"), and then in 1811 by Gabriel Franchere ("Thlakalamah") in his "Narrative of a Voyage to the Northwest Coast of American, 1811-1814". The name has no connection to the often stated belief the name came from a Hudson's Bay Company employee John Kalama, a native Hawaiian who arrived in 1837 and worked at Fort Nez Perce, Fort Nisqually, Fort Vancouver, and at the Cowlitz Farm, and settled in the Nisqually area in the late 1800s

1806:
In 1806 the Lewis and Clark journals mention the Kalama River. Lewis and Clark refer to the river as **"Cath la haws Creek"**, while Ordway calls the river **"Calams"** and Whitehouse calls the river **"Calamus"**.

"... to the Mouth of *Cath-la-haws* V Creek Std ... 9 miles ... I thought was a Id. ..." [Clark, winter 1805-06]

"... we proceed on to the mo of a River named Calams River and Camped on the South Side little above Said River ..." [Ordway, March 27, 1806]

"... We continued on & passed the Mouth of a River called by the Natives Calamus ..." [Whitehouse, March 27, 1806]

1811-1814:
Gabriel Franchere, in his "Narrative of a Voyage to the Northwest Coast of America, 1811-1814" (published 1854), mentions an Indian village called "Thlakalamah", located on a "small stream". A variant of the name is "Thlakalama".

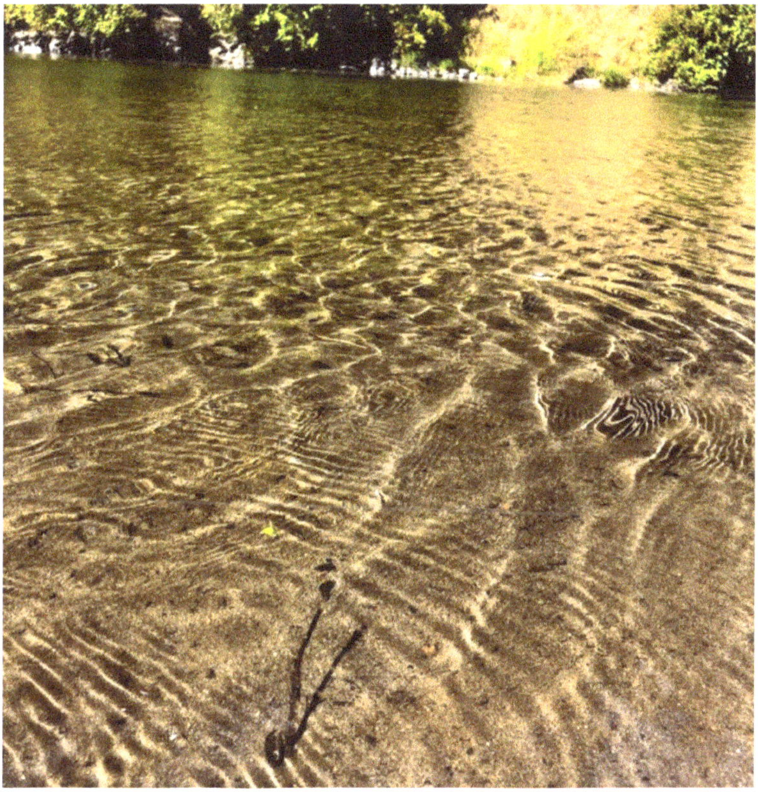

Access is limited. Obvious reasons. Crystal clear with fish.

"On the morning of the 6th we ascended this small stream, and soon arrived at a large village called *Thlakalamah*, the chief whereof, who was a young and handsome man, was called *Keasseno*, and was a relative of our guide. The situation of this village is the most charming that can be, being built on the little river that we had ascended, and indeed at its navigable head, being here but a torrent with numerous cascades leaping from rock to rock in their descent to the deep, limpid water, which flows through a beautiful prairie, enamelled with odorous flowers of all colors, and studded with superb groves of oak." [Franchere, May 6, 1811]

1805-1849:

Frederick Webb Hodge in his 1910 publication "Handbook of American Indians North of Mexico, Part 2" writes:

"Thlakalama. -- A Chinookan tribe formerly residing at the mouth of Kalama r., Cowlitz co., Wash. They spoke the Cathlamet dialect. In 1806 they numbered 200, but are now extinct.

Cathlahaws. -- Lewis and Clark Exped., II, 226, 1814.

Klakalama. -- Framboise (1805) quoted by Gairdner in Jour. Roy. Geog. Soc., XI, 255, 1841.

Thlakalamah. -- Franchere Narr., 110, 1854.

Tkalama. -- Gibbs, MS. no. 248, B.A.E. (Chinook name.)

Tk'ala'ma. -- Boas, inf'n, 1905 (proper name.)

Wacalamus. -- Ross, Adventures, 87, 1849."

Source: Columbiariverimages.com Thanks for the history.

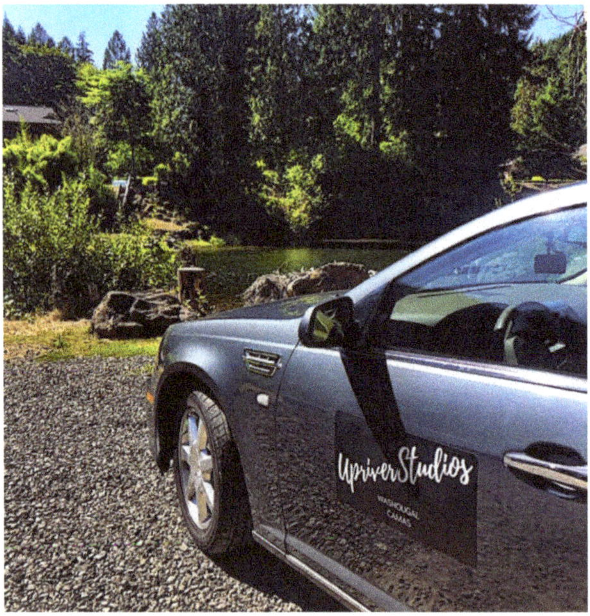

Buddy Love and I enjoyed the river. We took a swim and headed back to UpriverStudios. Kalama is so cute! Known for their antique shops. They filmed the movie "Twilight." here. September 1st 1957 Elvis Presley stayed at Kalama's, Columbia Inn. The locals still talk about it.

Kress Lake

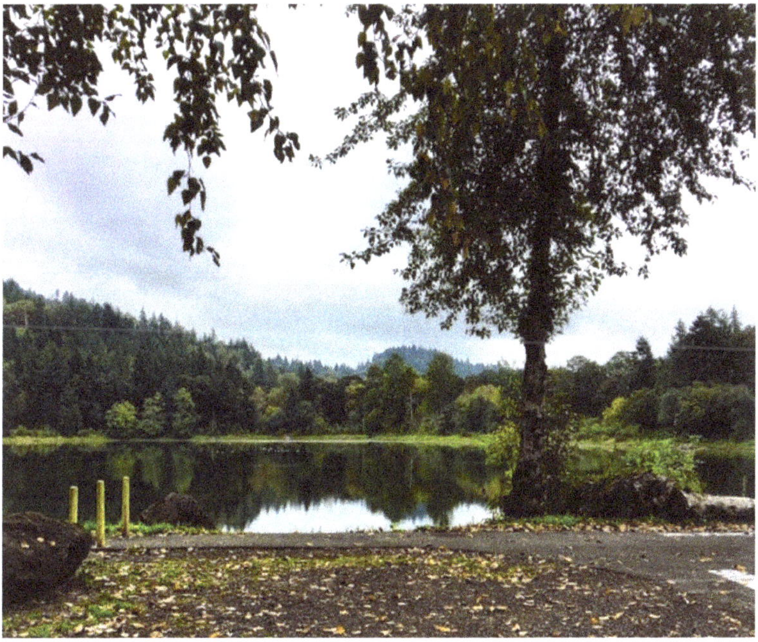

Wheelchair friendly Kress Lake is Just off of I-5 at Kalama River Road.

Kress Lake is an old gravel pit acquired by Washington Department of Fish and Wildlife in 1981. It is a popular trout and warmwater fish lake. Catchable Rainbow Trout and Brown Trout are planted from January to May and then again in November.

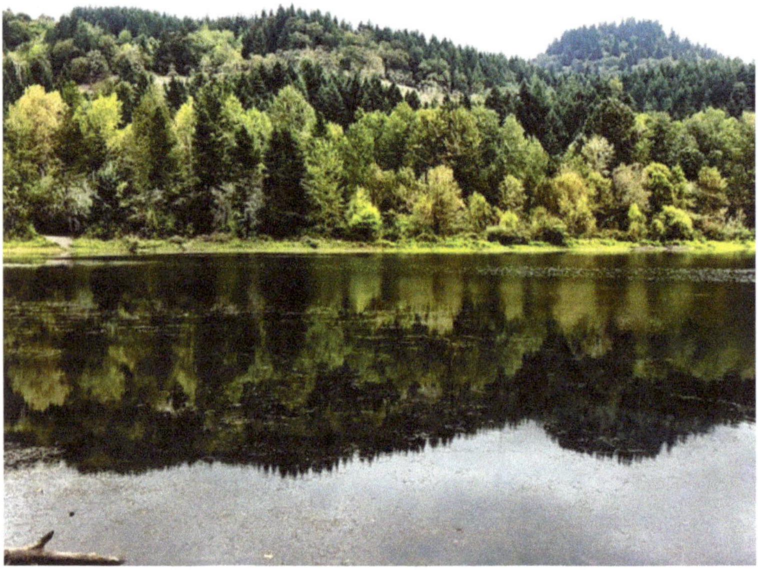

There is a parking lot with restrooms available.

Channel Catfish were first planted in 1998. The department has continued stocking Channel Catfish in subsequent years. Surplus adult hatchery Steelhead are occasionally also planted throughout the fall and winter. The pond has invasive Eurasian Milfoil making recreational fishing difficult at times.

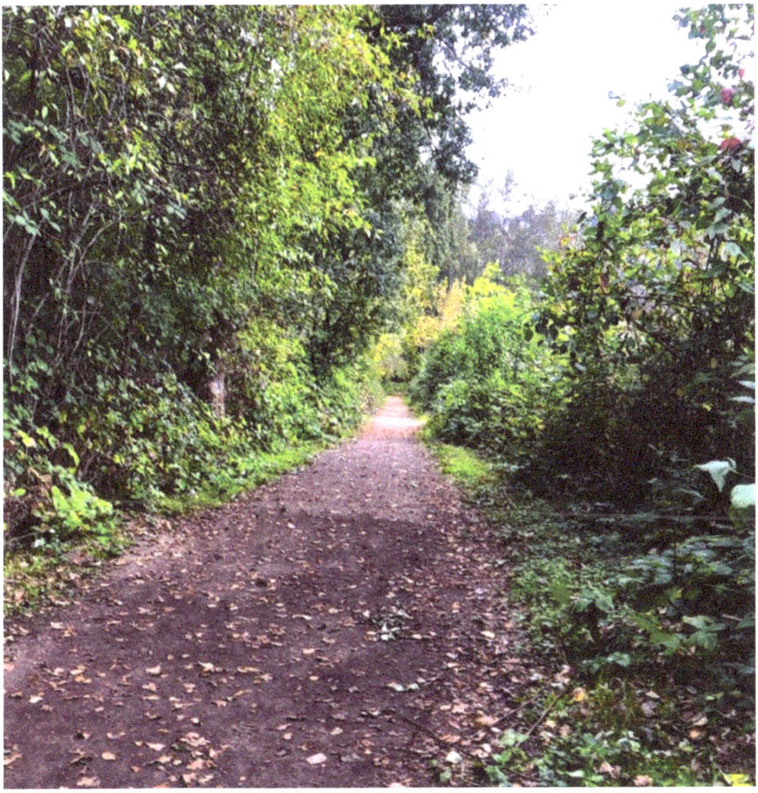

Trails are wide and go all the way around the lake.

Landlocked salmon rules allow anglers to take surplus hatchery salmon, when available.This lake provides an excellent trout fishing opportunity from late fall through late spring.

Gasoline motors are not allowed. Kress provides some bank access with a trail going around the entire lake.

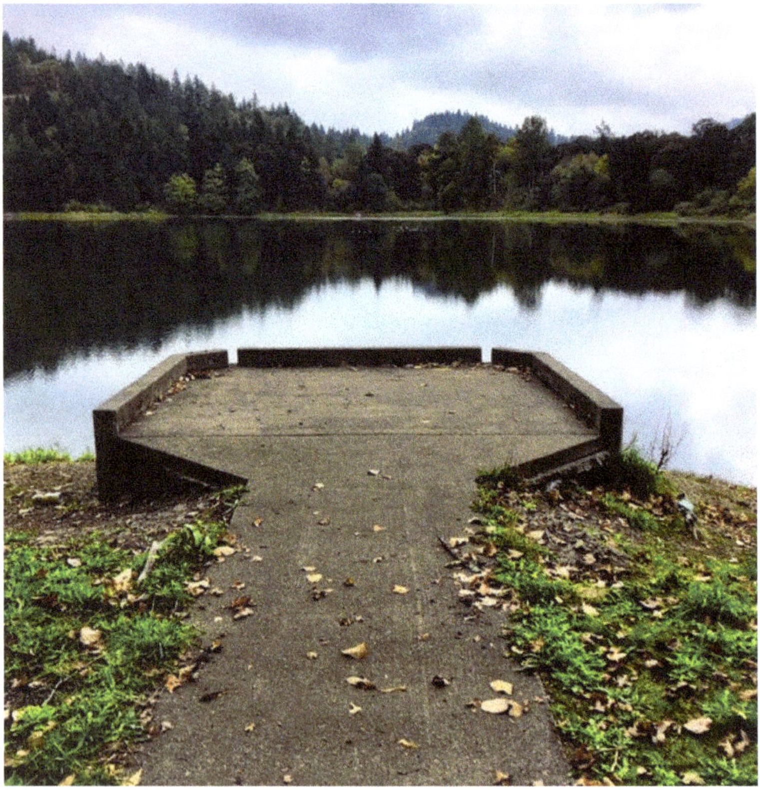

Wheelchair friendly dock at Kress Lake in Washington State.

Two-pole fishing **is allowed**

Shoreline access: Good
Good shore access for walking.

WDFW water access areas on this lake

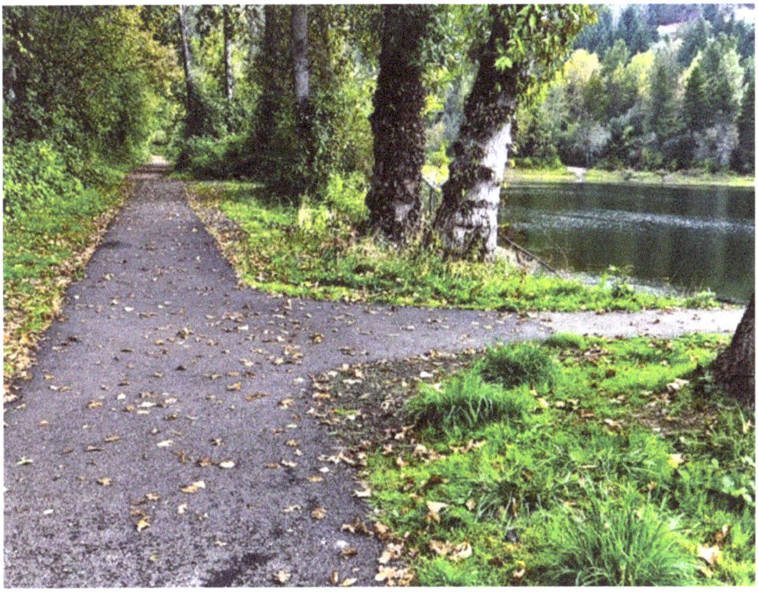

Fall leaves are starting their yearly show. It was calm and quiet.

Species you might catch

- Black crappie
- Bluegill
- Brown bullhead
- Channel catfish
- Common carp
- Largemouth bass
- Pumpkinseed Sunfish
- Rainbow trout
- Steelhead
- Warmouth

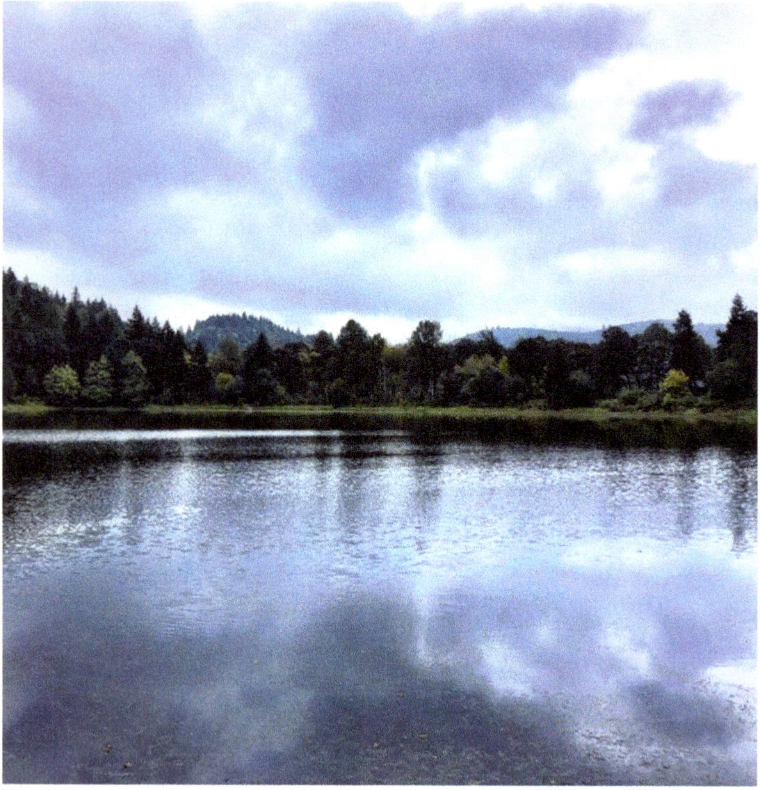

Pacific Northwest Fishermen, fish in the rain. October rain clouds were coming our way.

Lake information

County: Cowlitz
Acreage: 24.60 ac.
Elevation: 18 ft.
Center: 46.04705, -122.850953

Battle Ground Lake State Park

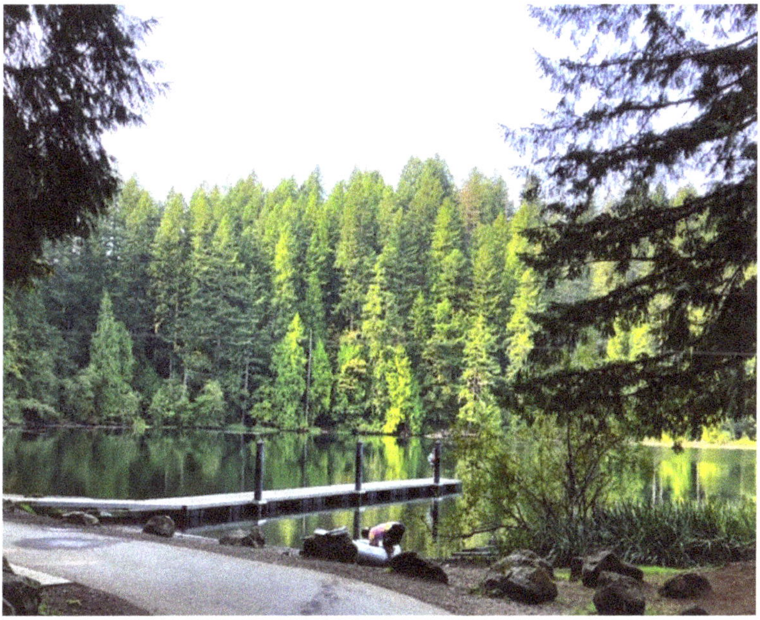

This day was calm and quiet enough to hear the children playing around the trails on the other side of the lake.

Battle Ground Lake is known as a crater lake. Initially Battle Ground was known as a popular crappie and bass lake. Rainbow Trout have been stocked in the lake since the late 1930s and have become a very successful fishery for anglers.

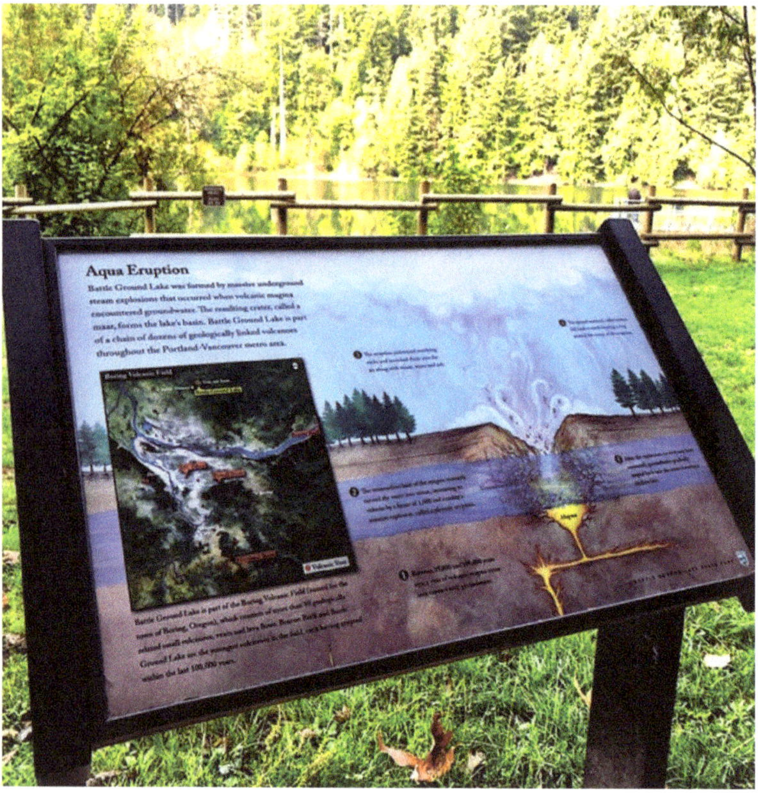

Aqua Eruption is responsible for this beauty. You are in volcano country.

Located inside Battle Ground Lake State Park about two miles northwest of the city of Battle Ground, off of Heisson Road. Thousands of Rainbow Trout and Coastal Cutthroat Trout are stocked during late winter through spring.

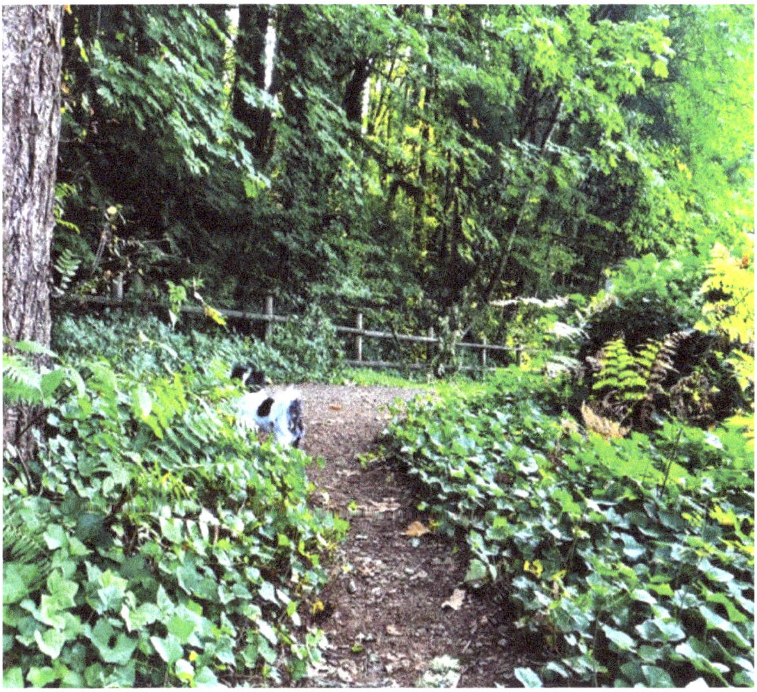

Trails go all the way around the lake. Bring a lunch, for the win.

The lake offers limited bank access and a dock (fee required) A Discover Pass is necessary to park at this lake. There is a small boat ramp, no combustion motors allowed. The Discover Pass is not necessary if staying in a registered campsite. Grass carp have been stocked in this lake. **Fishing for or retaining grass carp is prohibited.** Photo courtesy of Nick Mortensen.

Two-pole fishing **is allowed**

Shoreline access: Good
Limited shore access.

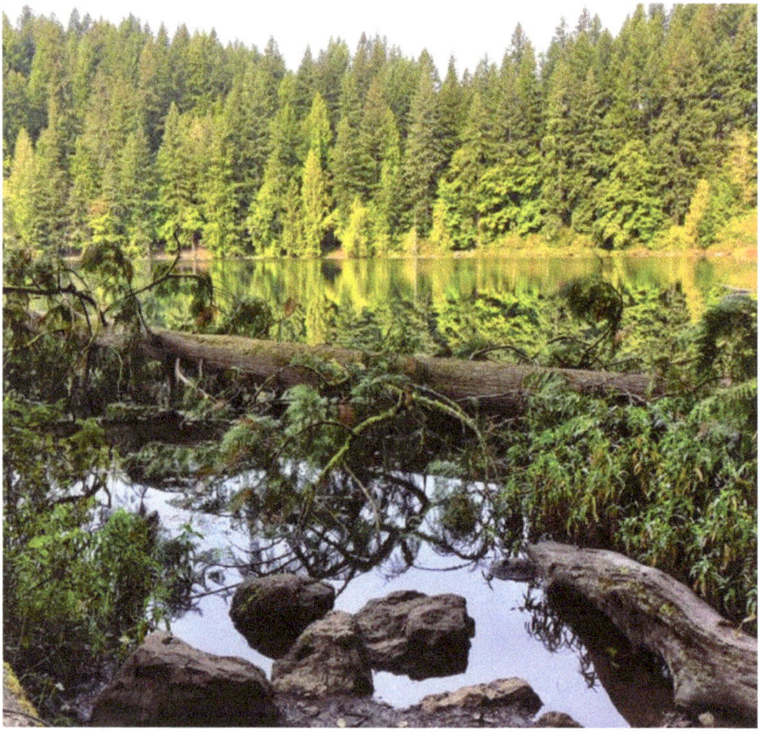

Fallen logs give perfect natural docks for fisherman.

Species you might catch

- Black crappie
- Bluegill
- Brown bullhead
- Coastal cutthroat trout (resident)
- Largemouth bass
- Pumpkinseed Sunfish
- Rainbow trout
- Warmouth
- White sturgeon

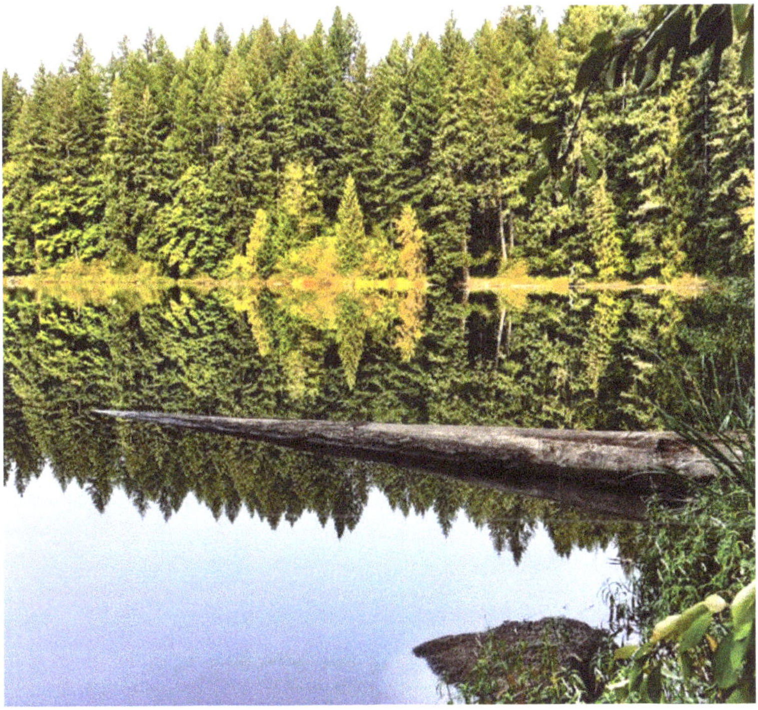

A local favorite and well kept secret. Clearly one can see why.

Lake information

County: Clark
Acreage: 25.40 ac.
Elevation: 509 ft.
Center: 45.804756, -122.494045

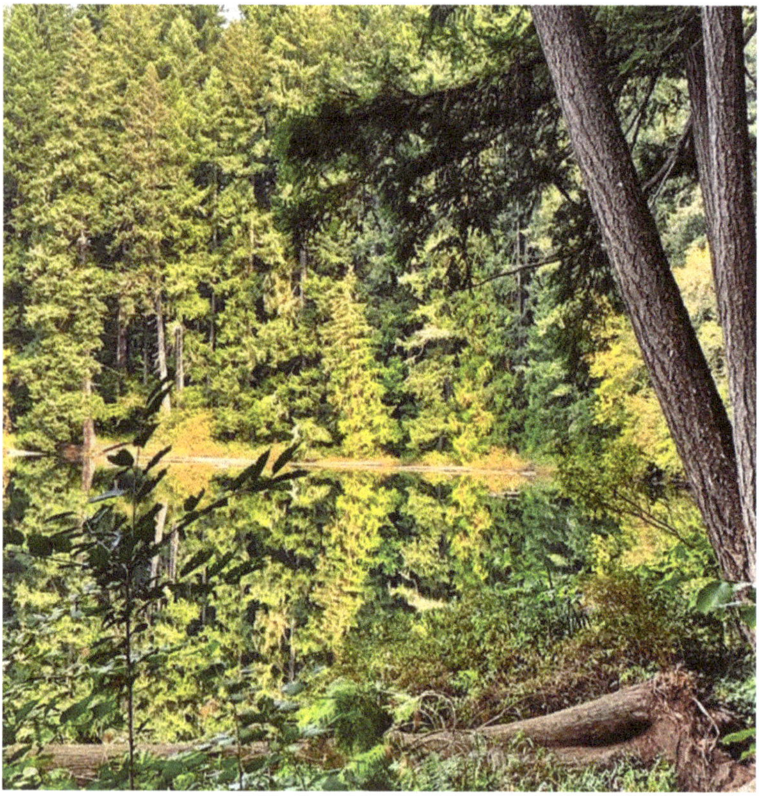

Battle Ground Lake this reflective October day was a natural mirror.

History

Battle Ground Lake State Park is a forested camping park in the Cascade Mountain foothills; its proximity to Vancouver and Portland and its cool green lake make it a great escape from the bustle of city and suburbs.

Children frolic in the shallow swim area under the watchful eyes of their picnicking parents, anglers float on the lake, hikers and campers take quiet strolls in the woods. On sunny weekends, laughter fills the playground, lakefront and kitchen areas. Whether you've come for a rest or a family play day, time spent at Battle Ground Lake will leave you refreshed and ready to tackle your life once again.

Park features

The 280-acre park offers hiking, biking, horse trails and a primitive equestrian camping area. The spring-fed lake is attractive to swimmers and paddlers and is stocked with trout, making it a favorite of anglers.

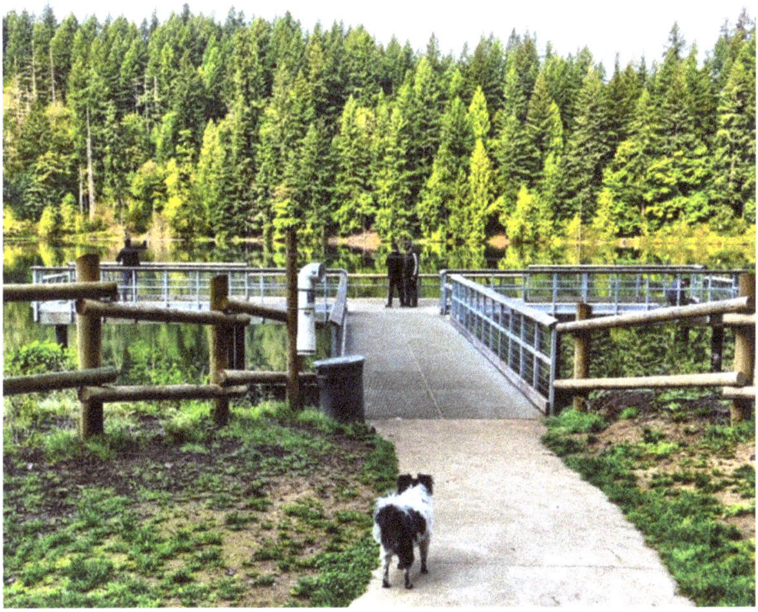

Fishing dock seemed to be the spot for conversation.

Discover Pass: A Discover Pass is required for vehicle access to state parks for day use. For more information about the Discover Pass and exemptions, please visit the Discover Pass web page.

Automated pay station: This park is equipped with an automated pay station for visitors to purchase a one-day or annual Discover Pass and boat launch permit.

1. Activities
2. Boating
3. Camping

4. History
5. Maps

ADA amenities/facilities

- Campground
- Day-use area restroom
- Picnic area

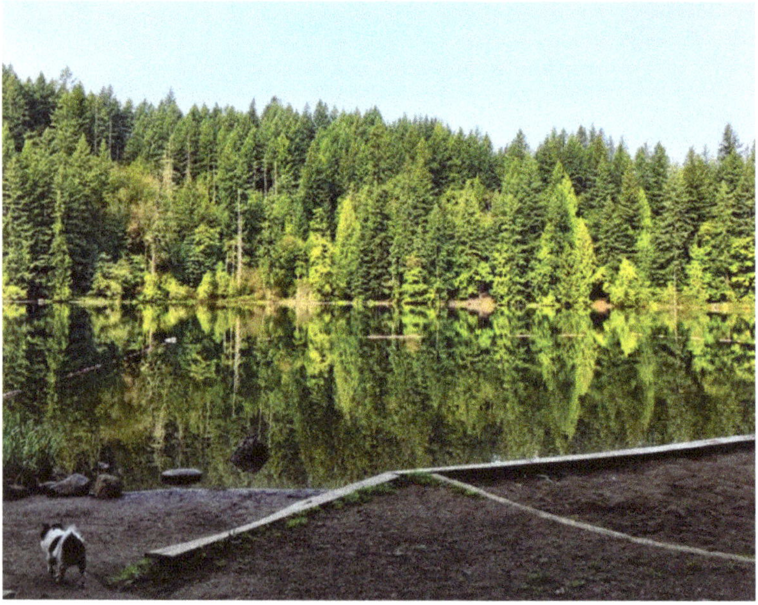

Battle Ground Lake Park Washington State USA

Use our interactive ADA recreation map to search for other state parks with ADA amenities and facilities.

Picnic & day-use facilities
Two kitchen shelters without electricity are available on a first-come, first-served basis year-round. Each accommodates about 20 people. There are 70 unsheltered picnic tables.

One kitchen shelter with electricity is reservable. The facility accommodates 20 to 150 people. Fees vary based on size of the group. Reservations can be made online or by calling (888) CAMPOUT or (888) 226-7688.

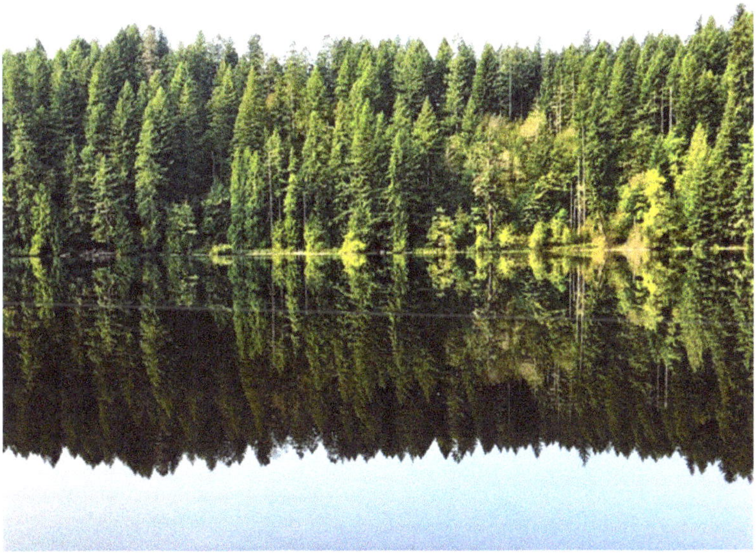

Great place to bring a picnic and your fishing poles. So peaceful.

Activities & features

Trails

- 5 miles of biking trails
- 10 miles of hiking trails
- 5 miles of horse trails

Water activities & features

- Boating (non-motorized)
- Diving
- 60 feet of dock
- Fishing (freshwater)

- Swimming
- Watercraft launch

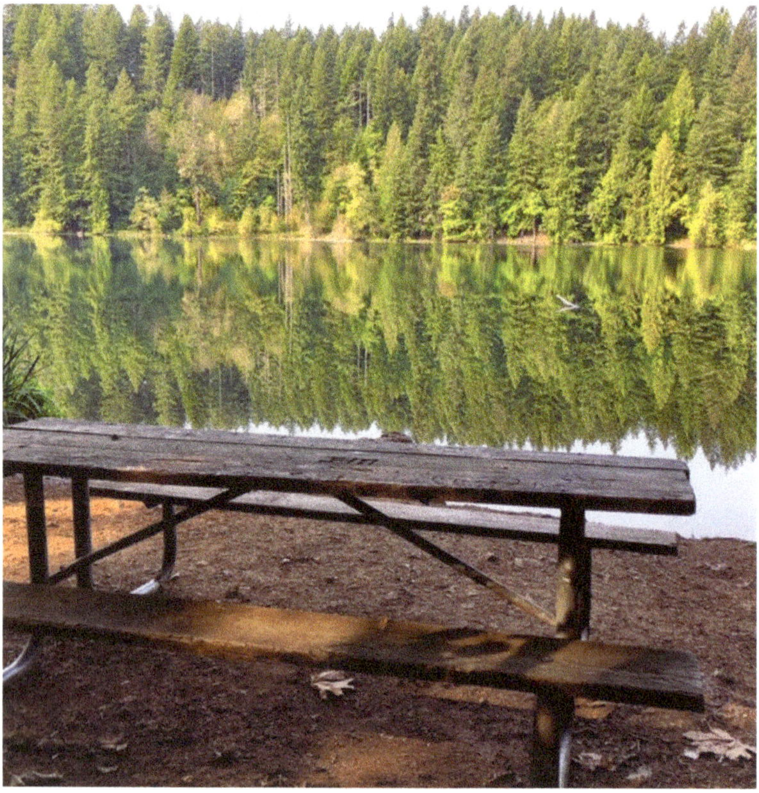

October's falling leaves of brilliant details paint the landscape.

Concessions: Paddle EZ offers kayak and stand up paddleboard rentals year-round. Rentals can be made on site or reserved in advance online. Rentals are located up the hill from the swim beach.

NOTE: Due to COVID 19 restrictions, Paddle EZ will NOT be available for the 2020 season. We apologize for any inconvenience.

Other activities & features

- Badminton area

- Baseball field
- Bird watching
- Fire circle
- Horseshoe pits (2)
- Mountain biking
- Softball field
- Volleyball field
- Wildlife viewing

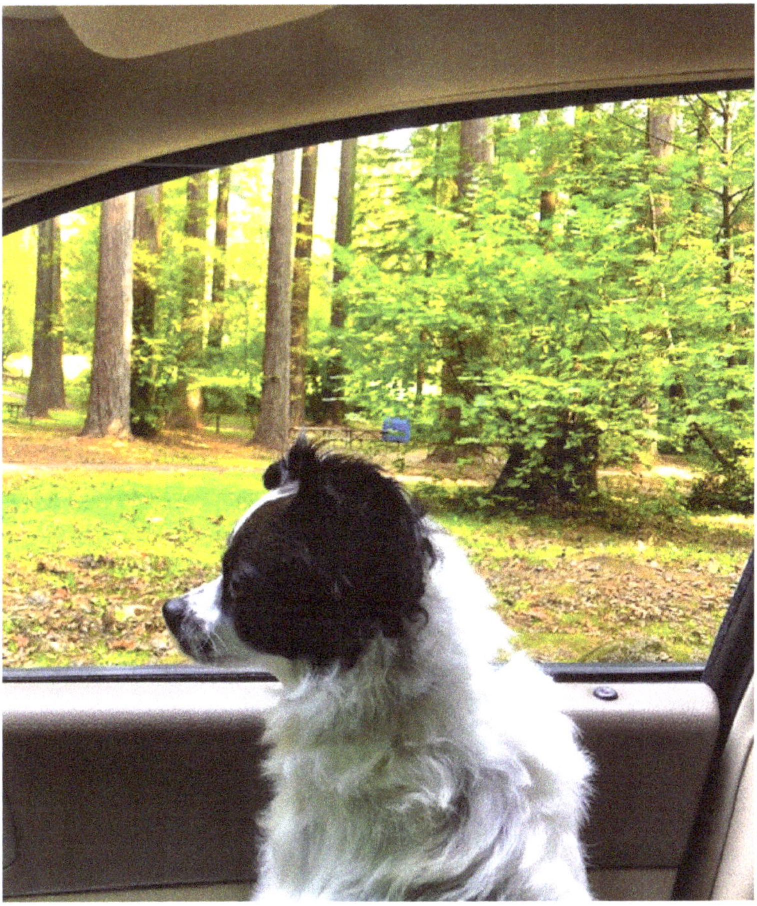

Buddy Love especially loved the campgrounds. He noted a bunny and squirrel situation.

Additional information

- The sports field has room for soccer but no goal posts. There are movable poles for badminton or volleyball. Groups provide net and ball or shuttlecock.
- The park does not have designated bike trails. Mountain bikers may use horse trails as long as they yield to horse riders.
- A recreational license is required for fishing and shellfish harvesting at Washington state parks. For regulations, fishing season information, or to purchase a recreational license, visit the Washington Department of Fish and Wildlife. Source https://parks.state.wa.us

Washougal River

The **Washougal River** is a 33-mile (53 km) tributary of the Columbia River in the U.S. state of Washington. Its headwaters and upper 21 miles (34 km) are in Skamania County in the Gifford Pinchot National Forest, and its lower 12 miles (19 km) are in Clark County. The river, which meets the Columbia near the cities of Washougal and Camas, is a popular stream for fishing, swimming, and boating.

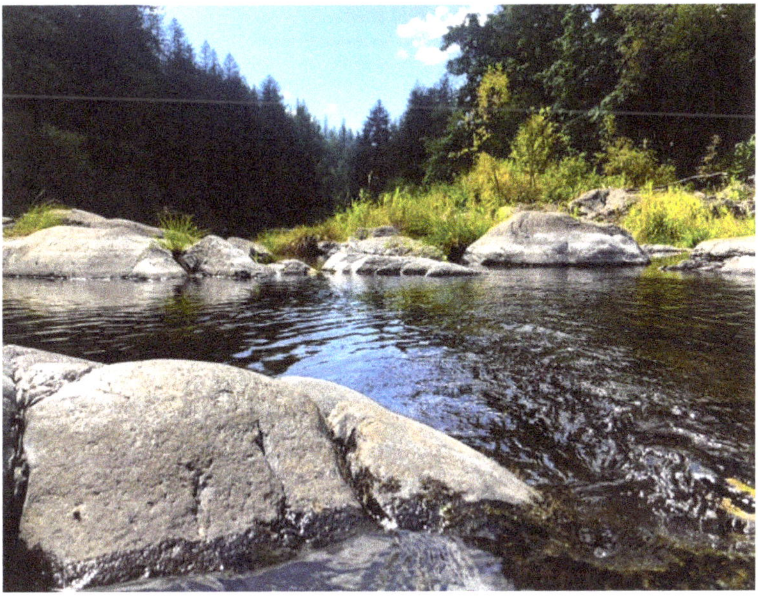

Washougal River in Washington State is a tributary to the Columbia River.

Explorers Meriwether Lewis and William Clark referred to the Washougal River as the "Seal River." The name Washougal comes from the Cascades Chinook placename *[wasiixwal]* or *[wasuxal]*, meaning "rushing water". It has been suggested that D. B. Cooper, who hijacked a Boeing 727 in 1971 then parachuted from the plane with ransom money, may have landed in the Washougal River basin

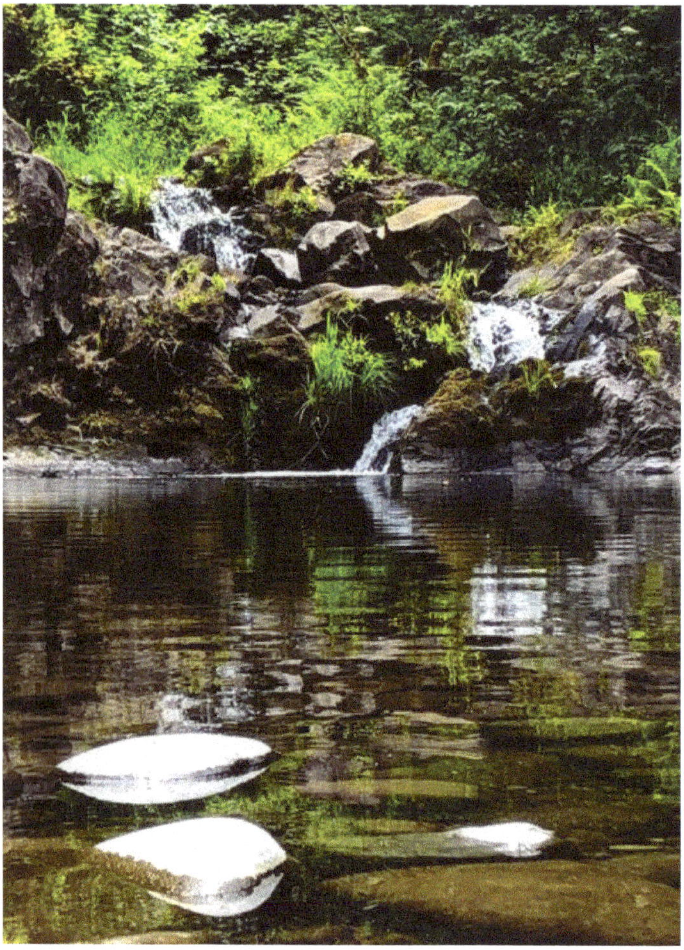

Washougal River is great for river rafting, SUP boards and kayaking.

Watershed

The Washougal River drains 212 square miles (550 km^2) of land that is largely forested, especially in its upper reaches in the Cascade Range and its foothills. Of the total, 162 square miles (420 km^2) are in Skamania County, and the remaining 50 square miles (130 km^2) are in Clark County. Small farms and rural homes are found along the lower part of the basin, and two small Clark County cities, Camas and Washougal, are at the river mouth. About 63 percent of the watershed is forested; 21 percent is devoted to fields, pastures, bare earth, and shrubland, and 16 percent is developed or cleared for development.

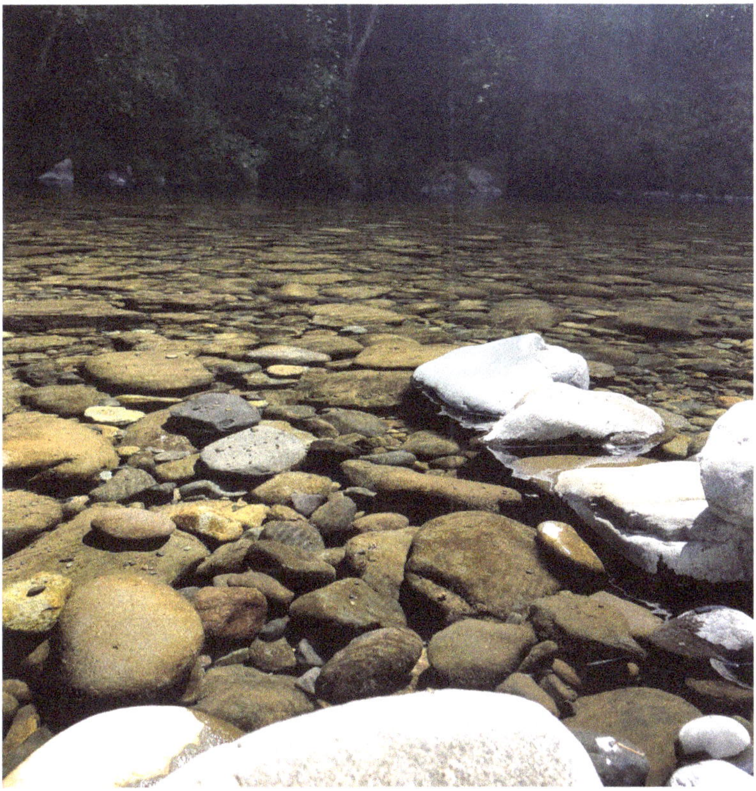

Clear and calm, we drifted for hours on a hot day. Wonderful.

The water quality of surface streams in the basin is rated "excellent" to "good", with a few exceptions. State and county officials monitor the lower reaches of the river for signs of trouble such as harmful bacteria, elevated water temperatures, and bank erosion related to forest clearing and other development. Two of the river's tributaries, Jones Creek and Boulder Creek, supply drinking water to Camas.

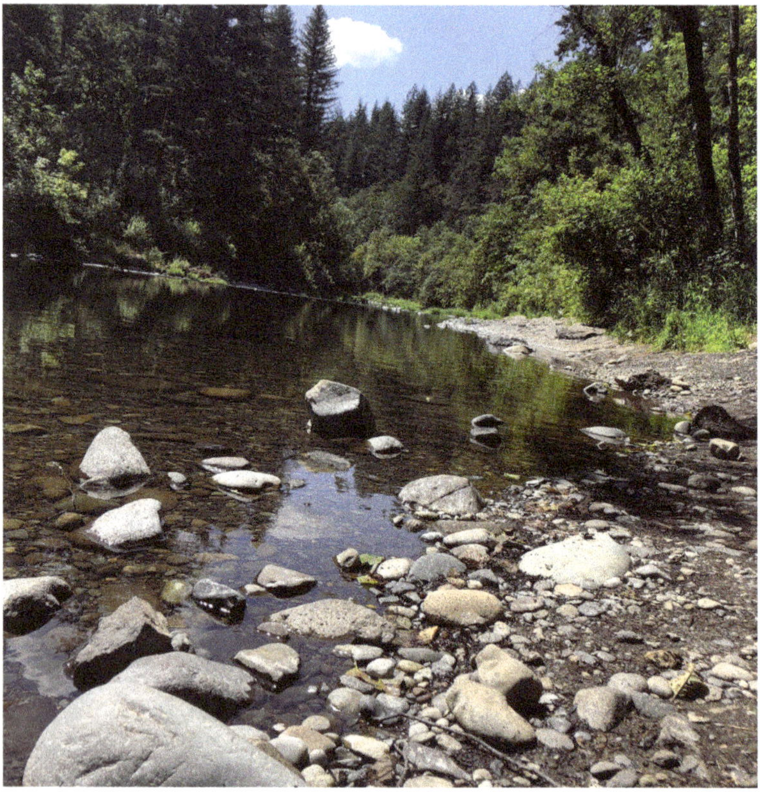

Perfect for swimming. Wear your river shoes. Washougal River in Washington State

Recreation and Fishing

The Washougal River, which has no dams, has significant fisheries. The main stem and some of the tributaries support populations of Chinook, chum, and Coho salmon, steelhead, and coastal cutthroat trout. Dougan Falls, 21 miles (34 km) from the mouth, blocks most fish migration beyond the waterfall. The Washougal River Greenway in Camas has fishing access, a short walking trail, a boat launch, and picnic sites. Much of the recreation access, including Dougan Falls, now requires a Discover Pass, Washington state's recreation fee pass. A separate parking pass is required for Naked Falls, which is on private land and was closed to the public for several years but has now reopened.

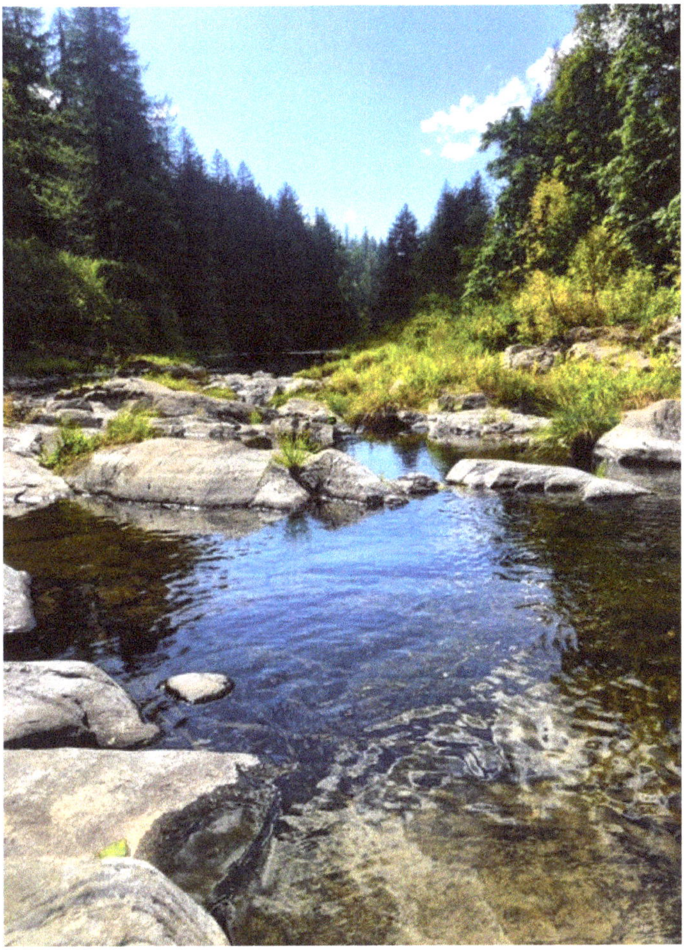

Natural deep pools on the Washougal River.

A series of waterfalls, some of them associated with swimming holes, are found along the main stream. From lowermost to uppermost, the named falls include Salmon, Dougan, Naked, Reeder, Stebbins Creek, and Docs Drop. Dougan Falls is a total of 30 feet (9.1 m) high and the largest drop is 19 feet (5.8 m).

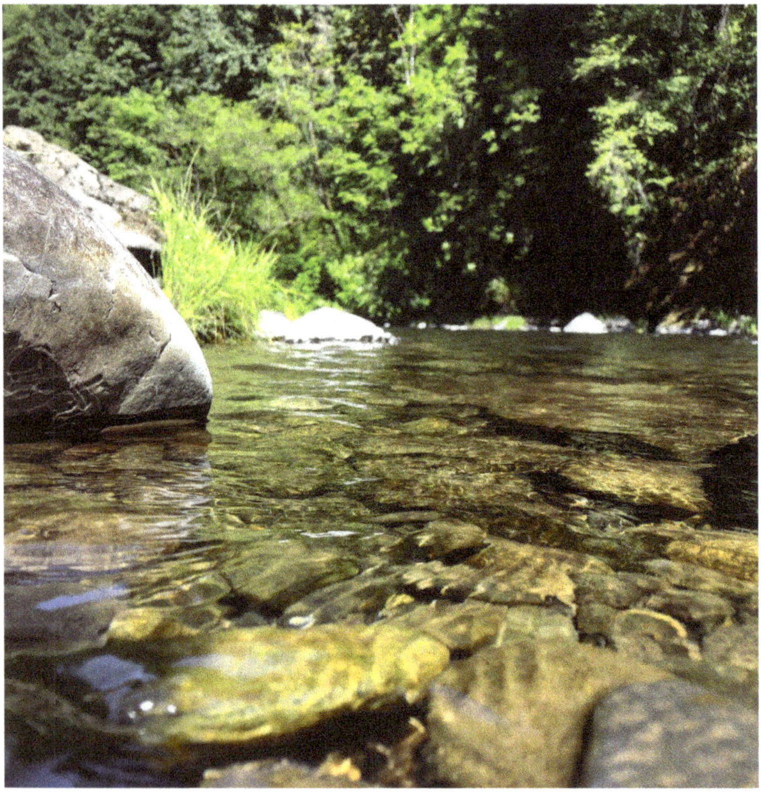

The river is where I go for cleansing the soul. I come away refreshed and with clarity.

Whitewater enthusiasts run parts of the Washougal River and some of its tributaries. The runs include many stretches rated 4, 5, or 5+ on the International Scale of River Difficulty.

Rafting The Washougal River

We live in Washougal Washington. Late July COVID pandemic 2020 the Pacific Northwest had a stretch of some triple digit weather. Darold patched up the Riverrat tube boat raft, we had decided to shoot the Washougal River. What a great decision. The river runs as slow as molasses. It should be called drifting not rafting. It was absolutely fantastic. Cold beer. A must do. The entire two mile drift took about three hours. Absolutely lovely late July summer day. The kind of day that seems to freeze in time. Sunburnt and nearing sunset, we went to the favorite local tried and true joint for a burger, fries and a chocolate milkshake because life doesn't get any better than that in a small town on a hot summer day.

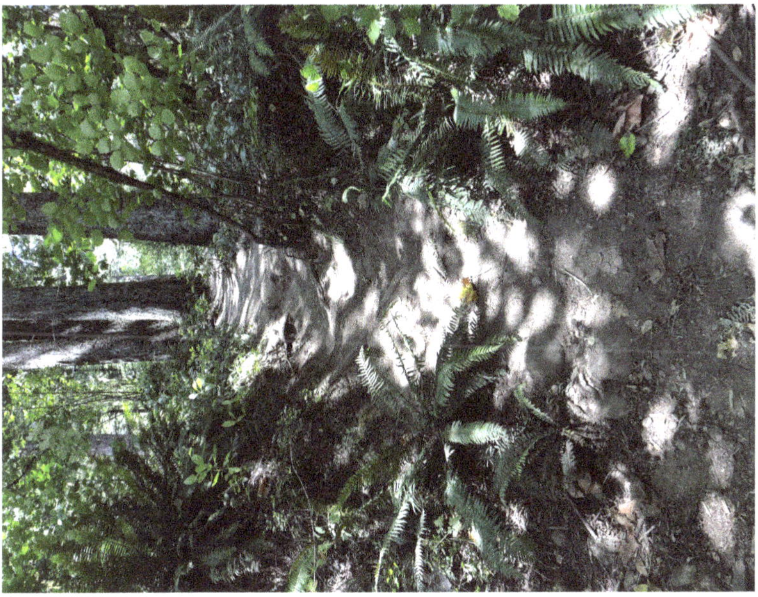

Wooded trail that leads to the Washougal River.

History of Washougal Washington

Washougal was officially incorporated on December 4, 1908. Its Mount Pleasant Grange Hall is the oldest continually used grange hall in Washington.

This small community is located on the Washington side of the Columbia River, with its lowlands and famous prairie situated on the west entrance to the scenic Columbia River Gorge. Motorists who approach Washougal from the west on the Lewis & Clark Highway can see Mount Hood rising above the Cascade Mountains framed by the columnar cliffs that signal the gateway of the Gorge. It is home to Excelsior High School and Washougal High School.

It can be accurately stated that Washougal is the "crossroads to discovery" in the Pacific Northwest. Shortly after Capt. Robert Gray, a Boston fur trader, entered the mouth of the Columbia River in May 1792, the famed British explorer George Vancouver traveled to the region to verify Gray's discovery. In October 1792, Vancouver directed a young Lieutenant named William Broughton to lead a party of men in a long boat up the Columbia to explore its head waters. Broughton came as far as present day Washougal and landed near the east end of Reed Island. He named Mount Hood after a British admiral and Point Vancouver after his commanding officer. Broughton incorrectly assumed the head waters of the Columbia originated from Mount Hood. In reality, the river originates some 1,000 miles to the north and east in Canada, but it would be 18 years later before the entire river was charted by another famed British explorer named David Thompson.

Captain Gray's discovery of the Columbia opened trade between Europeans and Chinook Indians who lived along the lower Columbia between the Cascade region and the river's mouth. U.S., British, Spanish and Russian fur traders bartered for sea otter and beaver skins in the late 18th century. Then, another important group of explorers visited the region in 1805–1806, but this group came from the east, which marked the first cross-continental expedition. These famed explorers were Meriwether Lewis & William Clark.

The Corps of Discovery was impressed with the fertile valley located near Washougal. In fact, when they finally reached the Pacific Coast and conducted their historic vote on selecting their winter camp site, the three viable options considered were the Clatsop area near Astoria (Oregon), the north bank near Chinook (Washington), and the fertile valley near the Sandy and Washougal Rivers. But, because the Corps had reached the Pacific in late November, they did not have much time to construct a winter fort before the cold weather set in, therefore choosing the Clatsop region because of the abundance of big game and its view of the Pacific—and they hoped to make contact with a fur trading ship to get word back to President Jefferson about the success of their mission.

On their return to the east, the Corps of Discovery rowed hard against the current hoping to return to the Nez Perce in early spring. The Nez Perce were caring for their horses over the winter and they needed the horses to travel over the Rocky Mountains. They arrived at Washougal on Monday, March 31, 1806. Lewis wrote in his journals that they camped on the lower end of a handsome prairie two miles up from the mouth of Seal (Washougal) River and directly across from the upper Quicksand (Sandy) River channel. By triangulating these landmarks, it places their campsite close to present day Capt. William Clark Park at Cottonwood Beach. The Corps would eventually camp at this location for six days in order to kill big game, dry the meat, and sew leather sacks in which to store the meat. Natives descending the river told them of scarcity in provisions (food sources) east of the Cascades. So the handsome prairie in present-day Washougal turned into a provisioning camp which became their second longest campsite in present-day Washington State.

So within a 13-year period Washougal would have famous travelers visit its banks from both the east and west—again in 1811 another famed explorer (David Thompson) would camp near the same "handsome prairie" on his famous journey to chart the entire length of the Columbia River.

In 1825, the Hudson's Bay Fur Company established Fort Vancouver near present-day Vancouver, Washington. Fur trappers and loggers began to visit regions of the Columbia River and they also assigned names to familiar locations. Washougal became known as Washougally Camp, which is thought to be a derivative of an Indian word meaning "rushing water." One of the first Europeans to settle in this area was a British seaman named Richard Ough (also spelled Howe) who arrived in 1838. While working at Ft. Vancouver, he met and fell in love with Betsy White Wing, a Native American Princess of the Cascades people. Her father, Chief Slyhorse Schluyhus, agreed to their marriage as a political alliance, but he stipulated as a condition that Richard must settle down. After their marriage in 1838, they stayed at Ft. Vancouver. Then in the 1840s, Richard bought a large swath of land near current downtown Washougal. He purchased it from a fellow settler for $45, a horse, a saddle, and a few loaves of bread.

Washougal was founded on part of the Oughs' original claim. Among Washougal's first and foremost citizens, the Oughs were generous with food and money. The Oughs had ten children in all, Sarah, Grace, Richard, Benjamin, Elizabeth, Mary, Fredrick, Cecelia, Emma, and John Thomas. Both Richard and Betsy Ough lived long and fulfilling lives, eventually owning a dairy dying at the ages 90 and 96, respectively. Both are buried in the local Catholic Cemetery and they have descendants who still live in Washougal. Personal belongings of the Ough's—including clothing and Indian artifacts—can be found in the Two Rivers Heritage Museum in Washougal.

Just downstream from the handsome prairie where Lewis & Clark and David Thompson camped there was a natural boat landing that later became known as Parker's Landing and played an important role for settlers following the Oregon Trail. Many pioneers coming out west would arrive at the Dalles (Oregon), where they would make rafts to float down the Columbia River. Dr.

John McLoughlin, the chief factor of the Hudson's Bay Fur Company at Ft. Vancouver, tried to dissuade American pioneers from settling on the north side of the Columbia River. He sent men to build barges and rafts to float pioneers to Ft. Vancouver, where they received food and clothing and were encouraged to settle in the Willamette Valley (Oregon). Those who did not want to settle in Oregon would float rafts to Parker's Landing, where a natural eddy would wash their barges and rafts up against the north bank. By arriving at Parker's Landing, they could travel to the interior of what would become Washington State, avoiding the British at Fort Vancouver who would try to persuade them to settle elsewhere. A well-known free African-American named George Washington Bush entered the state of Washington through Parker's Landing, and eventually traveled to the center of the state, where he founded the community of Tumwater. David C. Parker came out on a wagon train with Bush and both floated down the Columbia on rafts in 1845. In 1846, when the Oregon Territory land dispute was resolved between England and the United States and the northern boundary was moved to the 49th parallel, Parker was quick to file for a land grant, which included the popular beach landing that would later assume his name and become the marina for the Port of Camas-Washougal. In fact, Parker would apply to have a young, fledgling community incorporated in 1852, and the community would be called Parkersville. This is thought to be the oldest incorporated community in the state of Washington. But a new community was developed just one mile upriver from Parkersville, closer to the lowlands for dairy farming and logging. It is this community that eventually became Washougal.

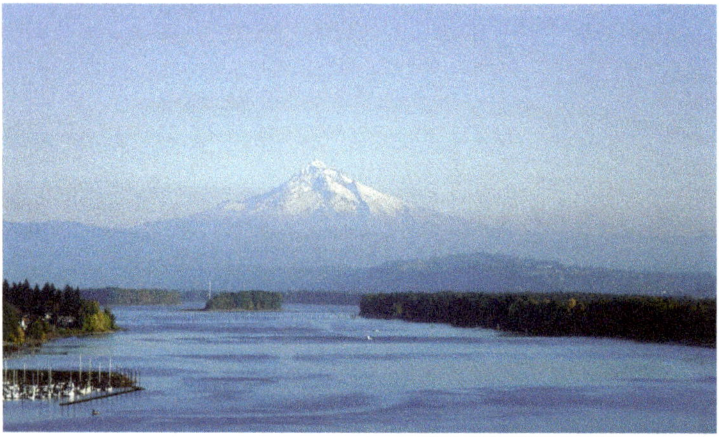

Mt. Hood overlooks the Columbia River. Washougal, Washington is the left bank and Portland Oregon is to the right. GettyPhotos This drone shot is great! She is majestic.

Dougan Falls

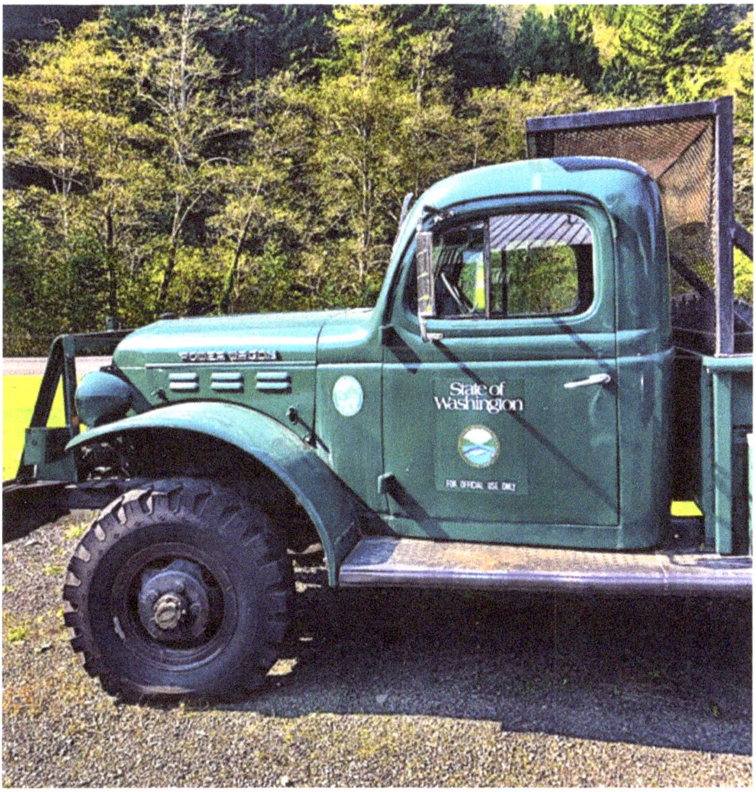

This old truck caught my eye while driving past the fish hatchery. My Family had a 56 Willy's Power-wagen boom truck in my Dad's shop. He was cool like that. I took to liking hot cars and rat rods at a young age because welding happens.

As summer goes on, the temperatures continue to soar and everyone needs a spot to take refuge from the heat. The final major waterfall along the Washougal River, the Dougan Falls can be sighted from a multitude of roadside stops. The falls are created as the Washougal River widens to more than a 100 feet and suddenly crashed sideways, down 19 feet, into a narrow trough. At the base of the falls there is an immensely deep pool of pristine clear water which is perfect for a nice swim on a hot summer day.

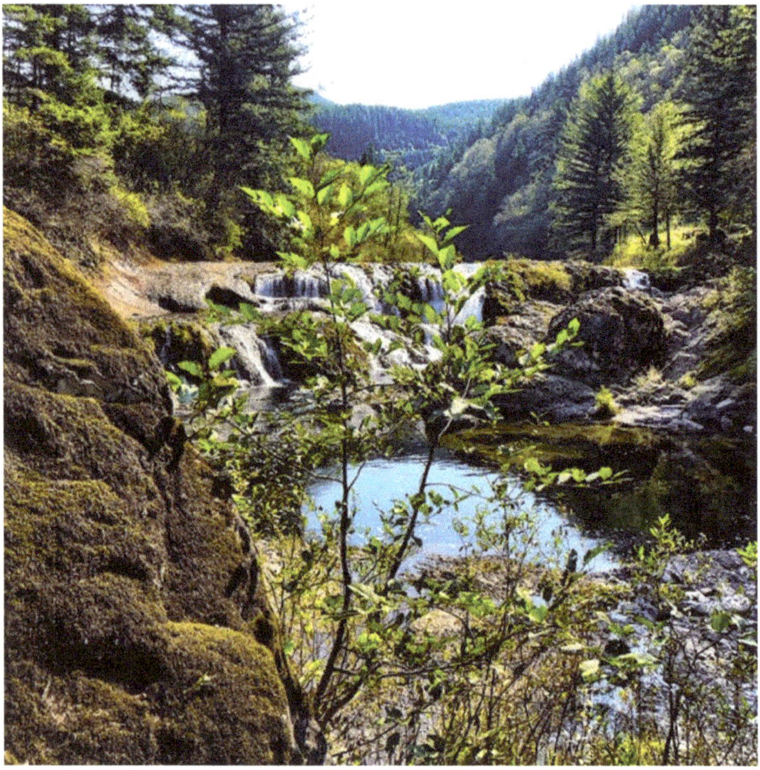

Washington State Washougal River Dougan Falls.

Among the best swimming holes located along the Pacific Northwest, the Dougan Falls are often ignored by Oregonians. Nestled towards the end of the winding paved river road, Dougan Falls offers visitors the opportunity to engage in a myriad activities. Besides wading in the giant pool of water, visitors could also choose to relax in the shallow waters at the top of the falls or lay out a large towel on the sandy beach just below the bridge.

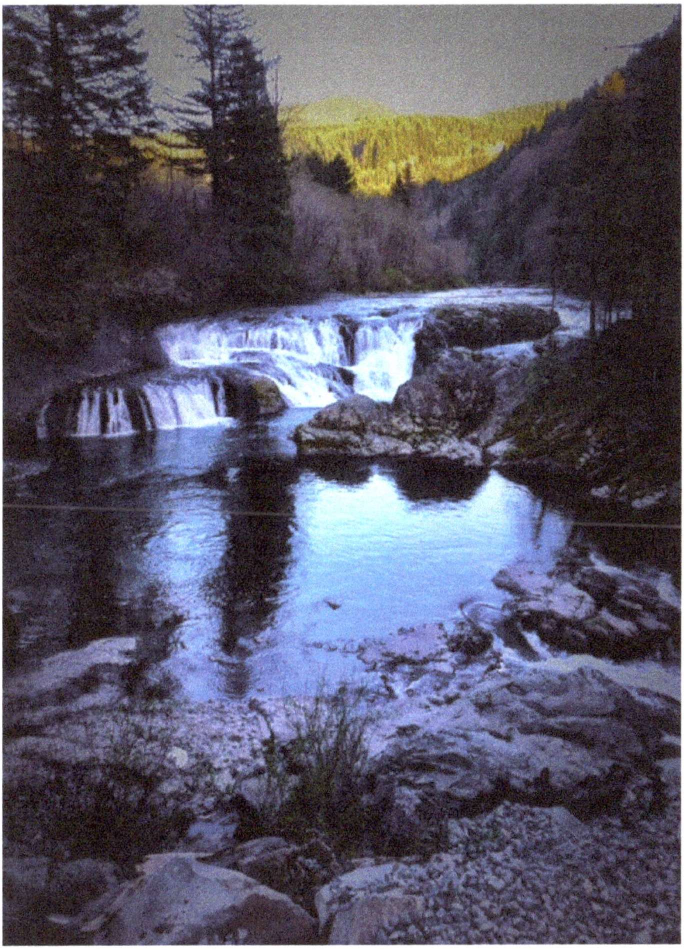

The mountain run off and natural rain water change the level of the Washougal River.

If you time your visit right, it is not uncommon to see many kayakers testing the waters. There are picnic tables in the day use area as well, making Dougan Falls a good spot for a family outing. Furthermore, the Dougan Creek Campground is located hardly 100 yards away from the falls affording visitors the opportunity to lounge along the river banks for more than just a day.

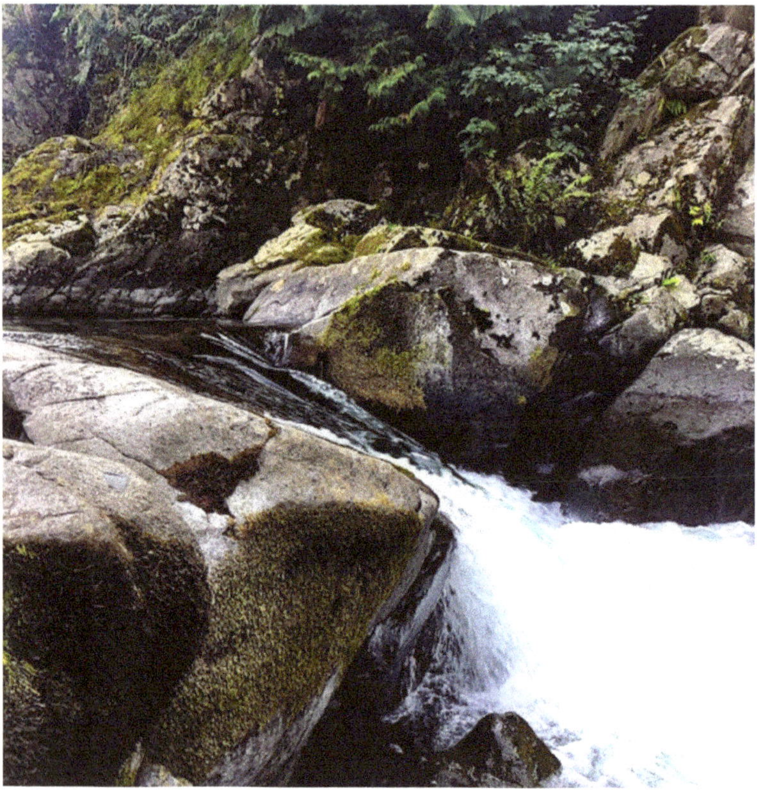

Photographers bring your gear. Every angel is a shot.

As one may expect, large number of people visit these falls making it a pain for those desiring a more secluded destination. That being said, a well-timed visit around the middle of the week ensures that you miss large crowds.

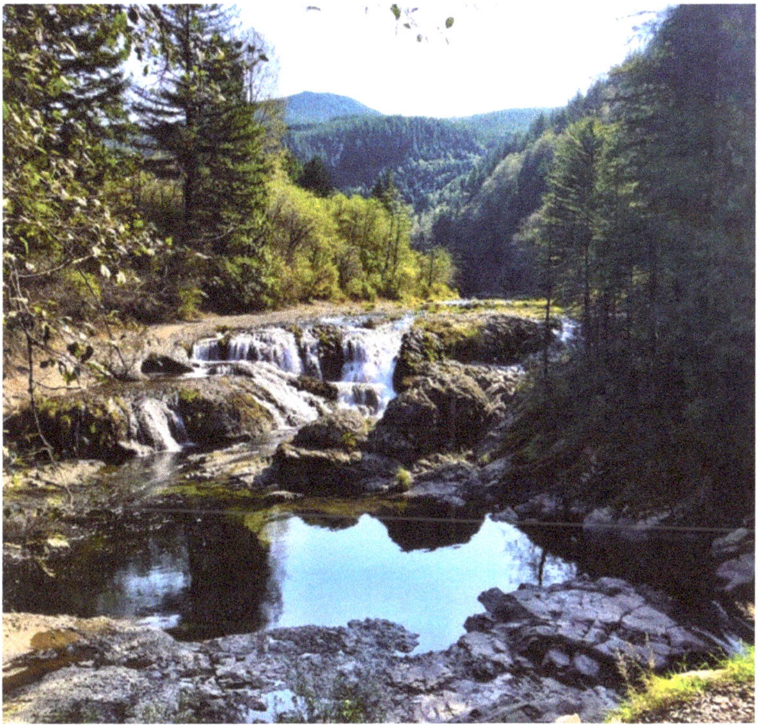

Dougan Falls in the beautiful Pacific Northwest

Dougan Falls Recreation Day Use site is a fee area. You are able to buy Discover Pass where hunting and fishing licenses are sold, via online on the site discoverpass.wa.gov, or over phone 866-320-9933. The annual pass is $30 and a day-use pass is $10.

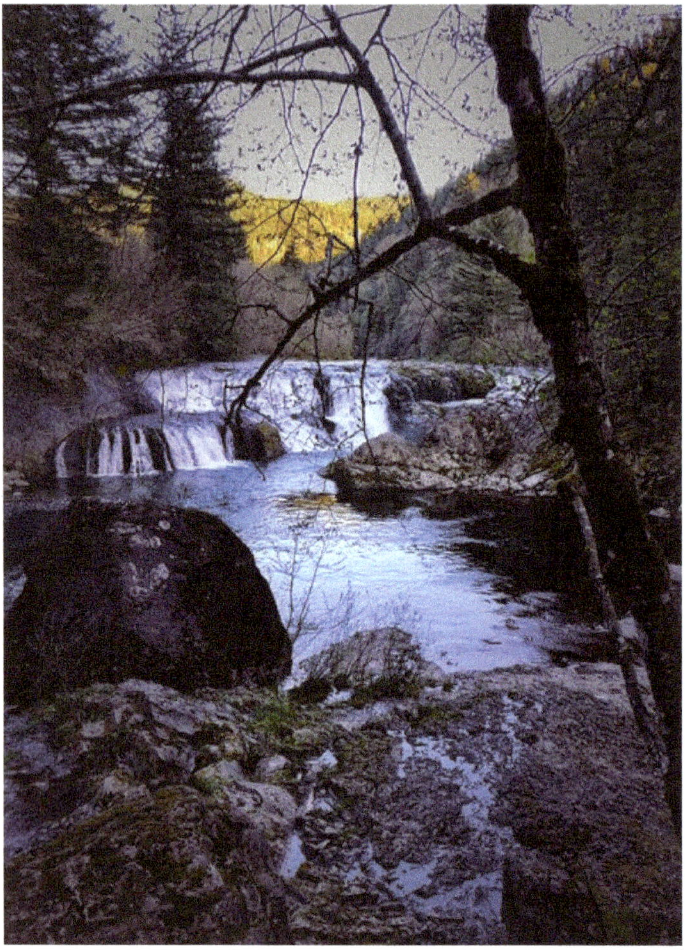

Washington produces more apples than any other state in the union. We're also first in the country for pear, red raspberry, spearmint oil and sweet cherry production.

Cautions: Cliff jumping and slippery rocks are associated with risks, please use caution and make safe decisions. Source: oregondiscovery.com

Dougan Falls day trip

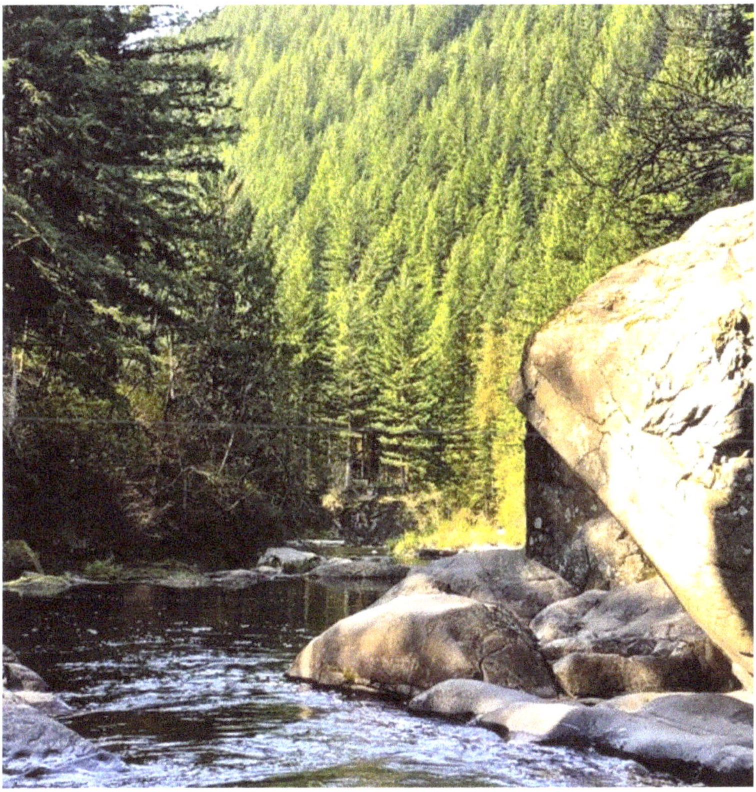

Washougal River below Dougan Falls, Washington State

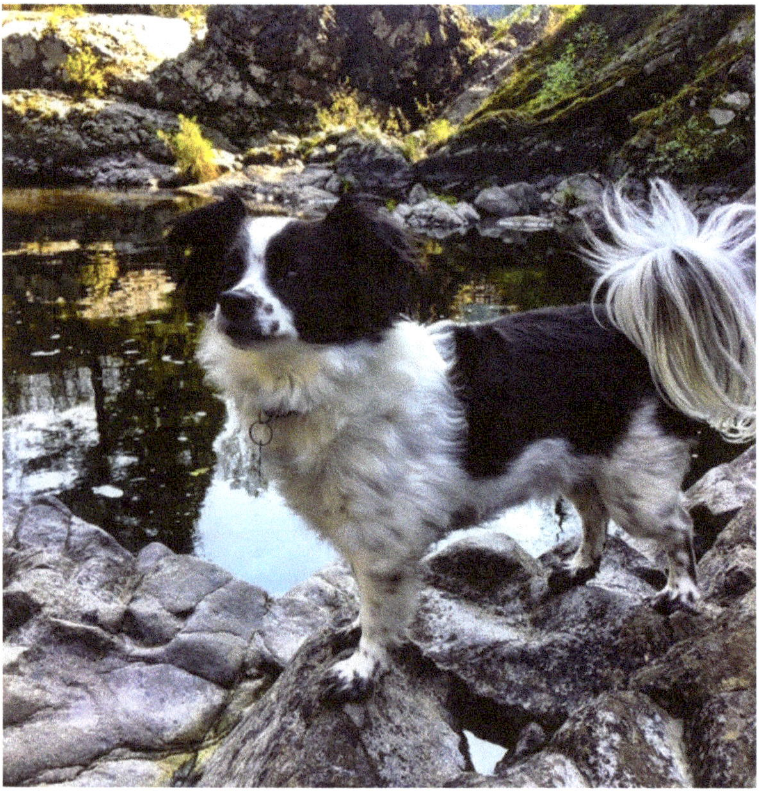

Buddy Love my sidekick.

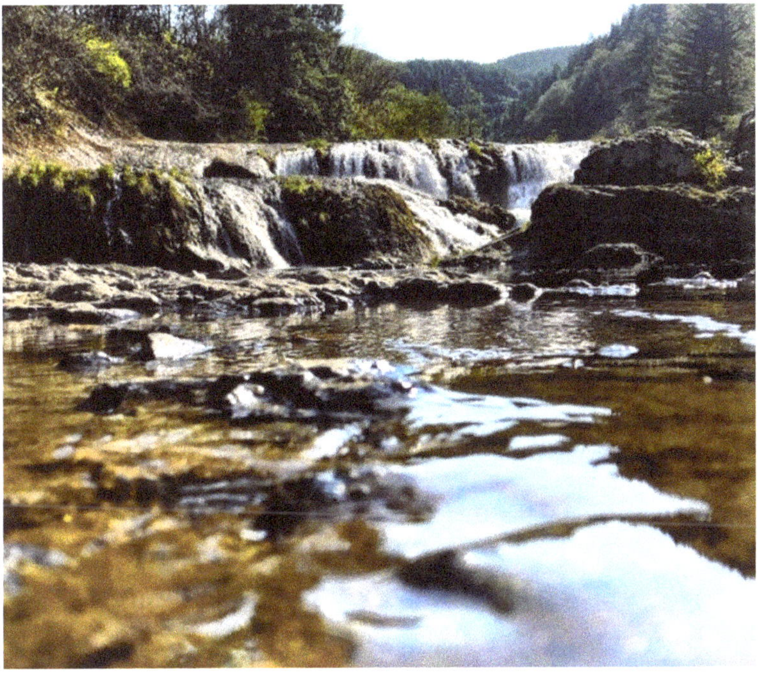

Best to go on a weekday. It can get crowded on hot summer days.

Winding roads lead to beautiful places.

This fir lined peaceful spot is in Washington State is a treasure. I find reflection and inspiration in nature, water and old growth forests. Nature is my life source. My meditation is feeling energy through the earth, sky, forest and water. The leaves had just began to turn to the amazing fall colors. So stunning is the backdrop of the Pacific Northwest. The mountain road is filled with pot holes, as the landslides are plenty in the high cliffs. Beware and pull over for locals. Rumor has it this spot was nick-named pot hole falls in the 50's. Must have been the hang-out! Beautiful.

Lacamas Lake

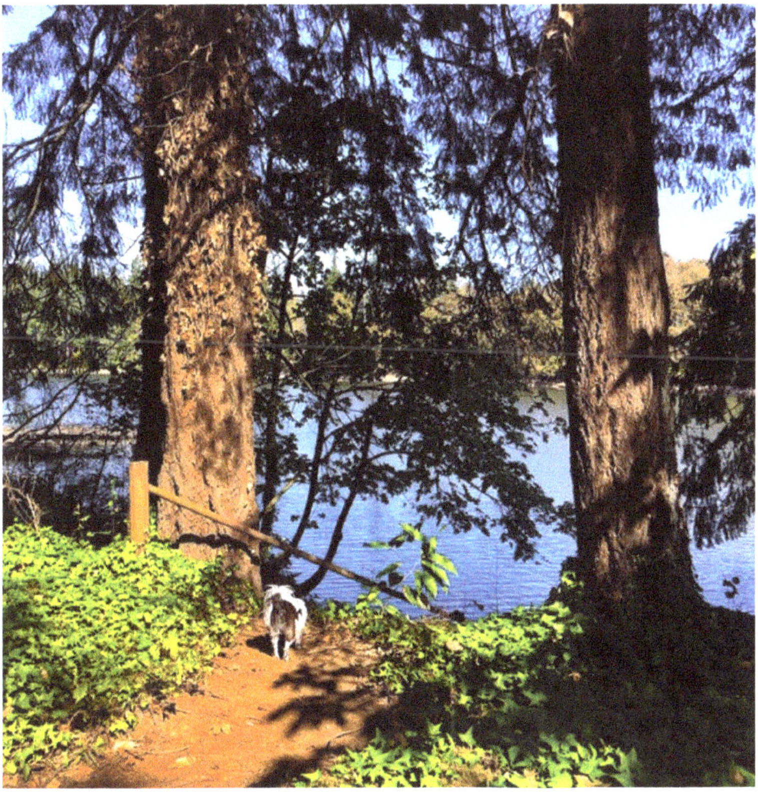

Buddy Love exploring Lacamas Lake Park

This lake was formed from a pre-historic channel of the Columbia River. The lake suffers from over-enrichment causing oxygen depletion, over abundance of plants and algae.

The lake is primarily stocked with Brown and Rainbow Trout; however, there is a good population of Yellow Perch and other warmwater species. The lake is located one mile north of Camas.

Round Lake, located at the southeast end of the lake provides good bank access for trout and warmwater fishing.

Two-pole fishing **is allowed**

Shoreline access: Good
Shore access is limited to the public.

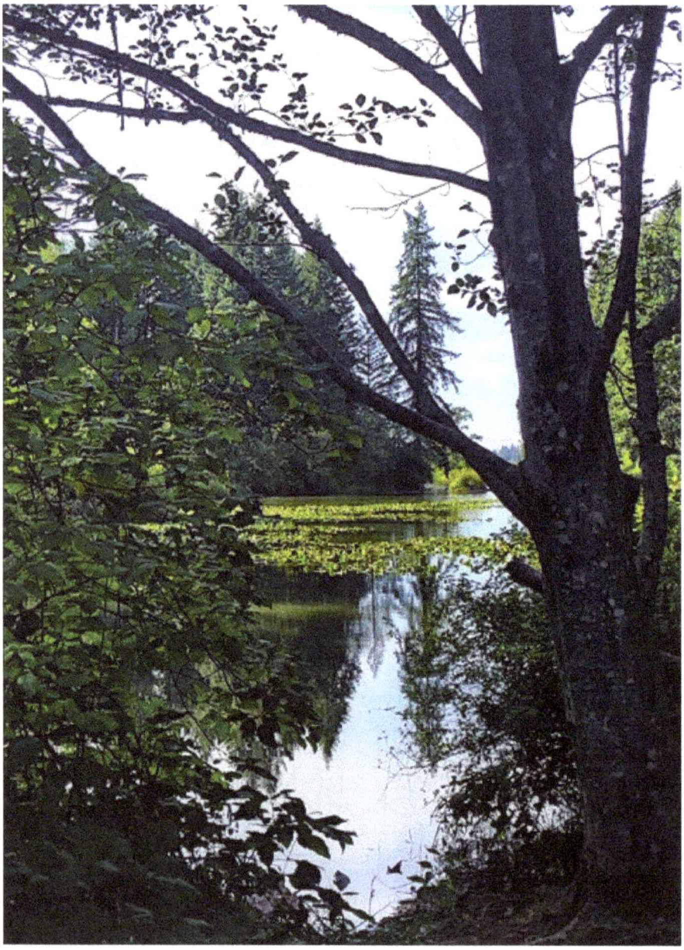

When the water is high the pond fills up. Great for SUP's and kayaks. Trails wrap around the park.

Species you might catch

- Black crappie
- Bluegill
- Brown bullhead
- Brown trout
- Channel catfish
- Common carp
- Largemouth bass
- Northern pikeminnow
- Pumpkinseed Sunfish
- Rainbow trout
- Warmouth

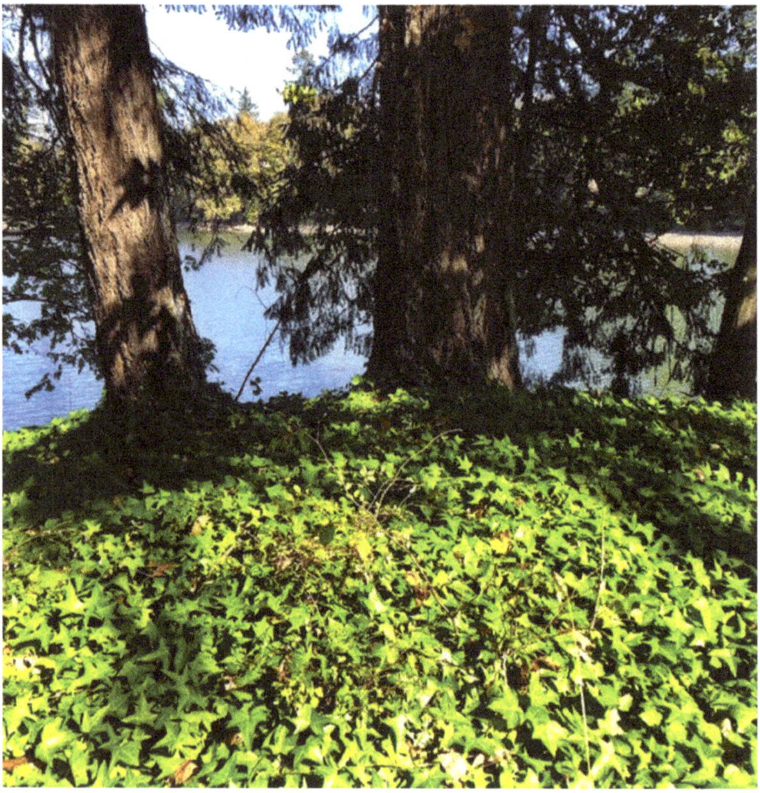

Lacamas Lake Camas Washington has many picnic tables and a playground with restrooms.

The Upscale Neighborhood

Lacamas Lake is a small lake in Clark County, Washington. It is a popular place to fish and water ski for locals from Vancouver, Camas and Washougal. It connects to Round Lake via a channel that runs under the SR 500 bridge on the southeast side of the lake. In the 1990s many high tech manufacturing plants and expensive housing developments began to appear in the area around the lake. The lake is very warm compared to other lakes in the area and the temperature can drop off quickly with depth. As it is now, the 60-foot-deep (18 m) lake cannot support life below about 18 ft (5.5 m) (see Dead Zone). The Georgia-Pacific Mill in Camas used to draw water from the lake to support its operations; however, Georgia-Pacific donated the two dams on Round Lake to the City of Camas in 2018.

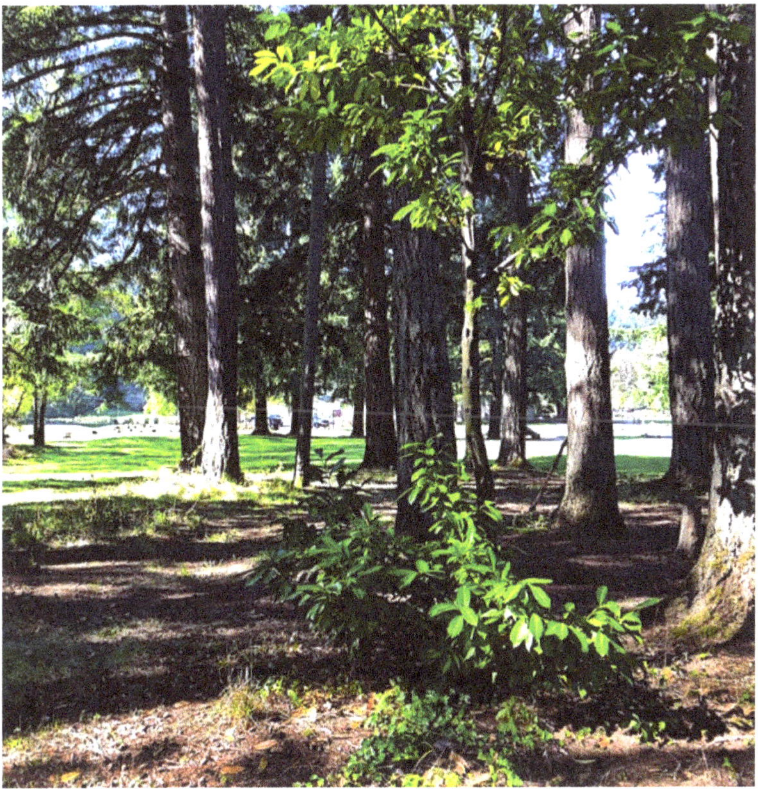

Lacamas Lake Park, Camas Washington

History of Camas

1883 LaCamas Colony Company selected townsite of LaCamas for their new paper mill. Mr. Henry L. Pittock, the owner of the Oregonian newspaper of Portland needed plenty of water to power paper-making machines for his newspaper and found it in the lakes behind the LaCamas region. The name "LaCamas" originated from the "camas roots used by the Indians for food" as written in a letter dated April 1909 by Mr. H. MacMaster, Councilman.
1883 Aeneas MacMaster opens the first store in LaCamas.
1884 First school and post office was established in LaCamas.

1889 Washington becomes a State of the Union.

1904 Telephone service to Vancouver was established.

1906 Camas was incorporated as a town.

1907 Northbank Highway opened from Vancouver, through Camas and Washougal, to Stevenson.

1908 The LaCamas Post, forerunner of the Post-Record newspaper, was created.

1928 The Crown Willamette Paper Company merged with the San Francisco-based Zellerbach Paper Mill Company forming Crown-Zellerbach Corporation.In WWII the Camas plant produced ship rudders in the machine shop. The rudders were being installed on the Liberty ships under construction in Vancouver and Portland.After the war, the plant's management became more interested in technical and research problems.

1946 the Central Research and Technical Department was formed to focus on projects with longer range benefits for the company and surrounding community.

1960 The name was changed to Central Research. In later years, Crown Zellerbach Corporations changes ownership and name several times - currently being merged, but known as James River Corporation, it is now known as Georgia Pacific.

2006 The City celebrated its 100 year's as an incorporated city.

Today's downtown theme consists of flower baskets, trees and landscape flower beds. New lighting was installed in 2001 and has been a welcomed enhancement. The industrial base has changed dramatically from a small "mill town" base to a thriving industrial park which benefits for its close proximity to the Portland International Airport, Columbia River, and surrounding large Metro area. https://www.cityofcamas.us

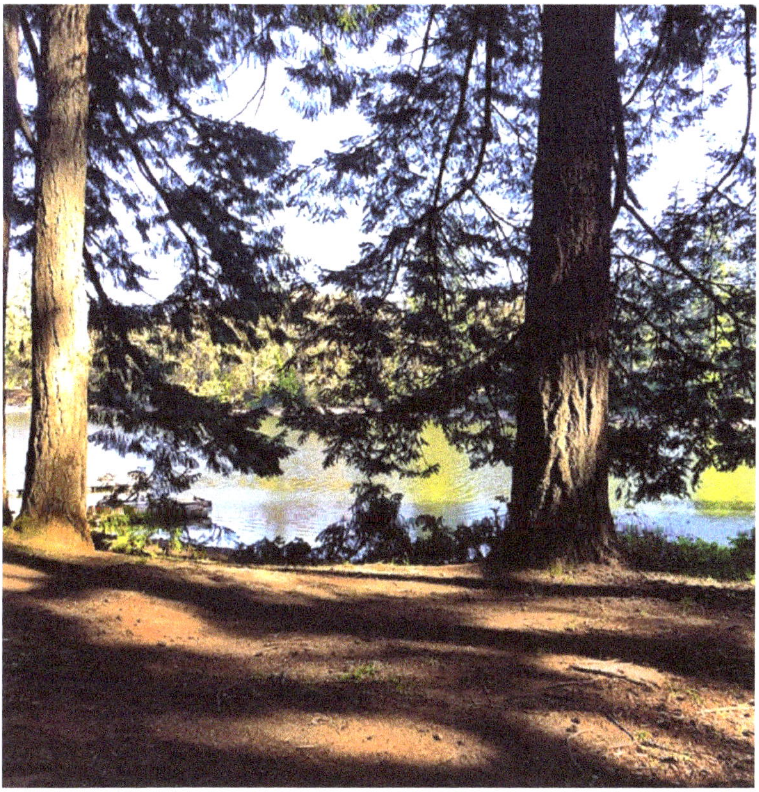

2020 Trout Derby. Camas is such a c little town. Pubs, restaurants and shopping are fantastic in Camas Washington.

Columbia River

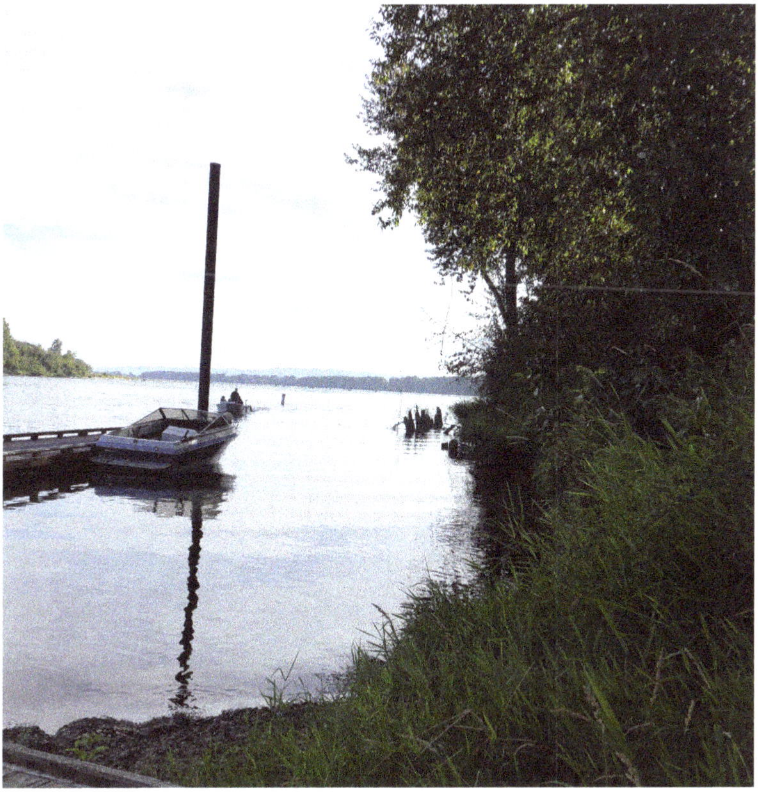

Fall Coho's were running on the Columbia. Her real name is Nch'i-Wana.The Sahaptin word for the Columbia was "Nch'i-Wana," the "Great River."

The Launch

We launched in a local well known secret spot. You have to know somebody. The weather was perfect and the fish were running. The Columbia River banks all along both sides of St. Helens, Oregon and Woodland Washington were packed with avid and experienced Fishermen. You could feel the excitement when someone had a, “fish-on!” If the locals are fishing like this, chances are the fish are running up the river. Competition is fierce. Keep in mind, they know you are not a local. Truth is they don't want you there. It's the spot their family has fished for five generations so heads up. Everywhere I have traveled, I kept this tradition in mind and had great respect for the local traditions. It starts with etiquette. Thank you Brother Dan for this advice years ago. Living on the river and with respect, I slowly made friends and they taught me everything.

The new electronic gadgets available for fishermen today are amazing. Fish Finders, depth readers, heated hip waders, polarized sunglasses. We launched near Woodland Washington, Home of two world famous fishing Stores. G.Loomis, fly and conventional state of the art fishing gear. and Lamiglas, “Premium Fishing Rods & Blanks Since 1949”. Both make great quality products and have cool stickers. They are both top of the line.

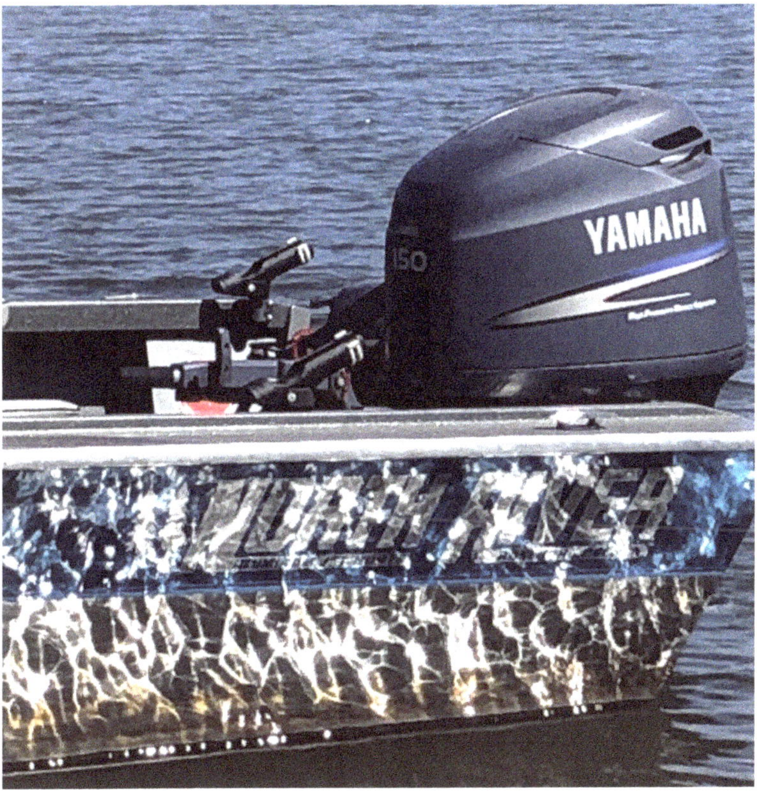

Brother Dan's North River has made a few runs in her day! The Memories are beautiful, life lasting and priceless. Enjoying the fruits of your own harvest is the rich life.

Tidal Rivers

A **tidal river** is a river whose flow and level are influenced by tides. A section of a larger river affected by the tides is a tidal reach, but it may sometimes be considered a tidal river if it has been given a separate name.

Generally, tidal rivers are short rivers with relatively low discharge rates but high overall discharge, which generally implies a shallow river with a large coastal mouth. In some cases, high tides impound downstream flowing freshwater, reversing the flow and increasing the water level of the lower section of river, forming large estuaries. High tides can be noticed as far as 100 kilometres (62 mi) upstream. Washington and Oregon's Columbia River and tributaries is one such river for which that effect can be noticed.

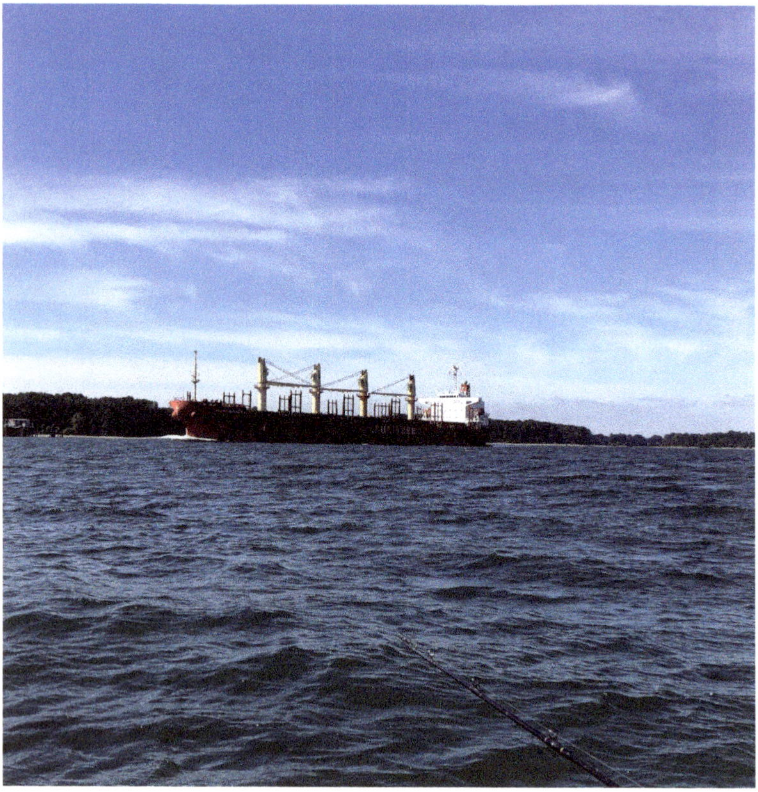

Majestic Ships float the Columbia, with Tug boats to boot. Somewhat of a parade.

Columbia River, largest river flowing into the Pacific Ocean from North America. It is exceeded in discharge on the continent only by the Mississippi, St. Lawrence, and Mackenzie rivers. The Columbia is one of the world's greatest sources of hydroelectric power and, with its tributaries, represents a third of the potential hydropower of the United States. In addition, its mouth provides the first deepwater harbour north of San Francisco. Two-fifths of the river's course, some 500 miles (800 km) of its 1,240-mile (2,000-km) length, lies in Canada, between its headwaters in British Columbia and the U.S. border.

Source: Marion E. Marts of Emeritus Professor of Geography, University of Washington, Seattle. britannica.com

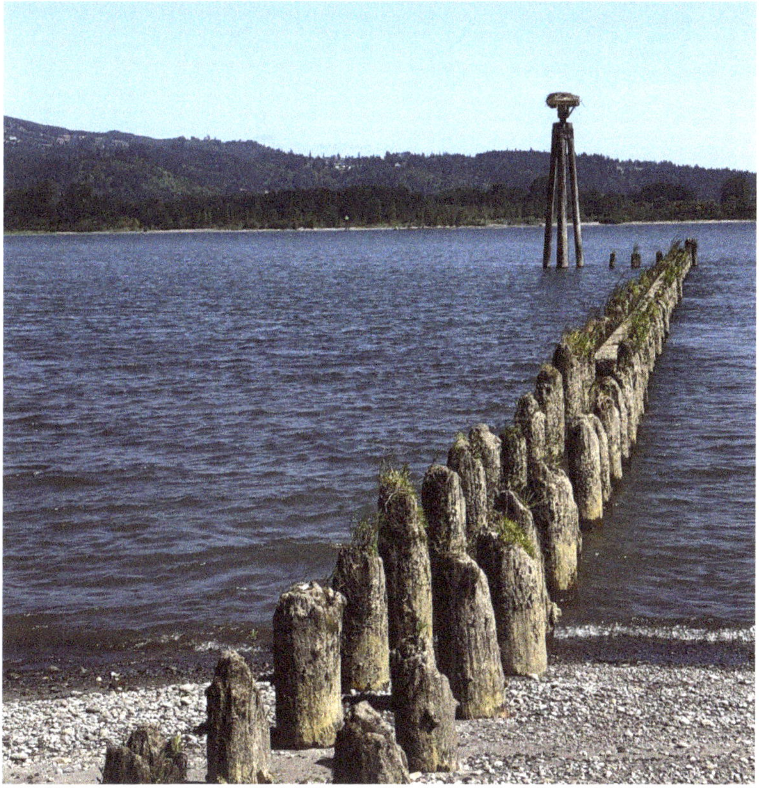

What are these?

US Army Corps of Engineers About our Dikes

The Corps has 233 pile dikes (also known as wing dams) in the 145 miles between the Mouth of the Columbia River and Bonneville Dam. Pile dikes were constructed in stages from 1885 to 1969. If each pile dike was placed end to end, they'd span more than 45 miles! Other privately owned pile structures are also in the Columbia River, but most Corps pile dikes are recognizable by the features shown here. The structure consists of alternating timber piles supported by a horizontal spreader. The king pile is a tall bundle of piles marking the end of the pile dike for better visibility. Stone blankets the entire length of the pile dike around the base. Corps pile dike structures in the Columbia River are authorized as part of the navigation projects, and help maintain navigation channels by directing river flow toward the main channel, resulting in:

- Reduced dredging requirements
- Increased channel stabilization
- Increased bank protection, including protection of dredged material placement sites

SAFETY MESSAGE: The tops of Corps pile dikes in the Columbia River are frequently just below the river surface during high water events and can seriously damage to vessels trying to transit over them. Many pile dikes are missing the tall king piles which increase visibility to boaters. Pile dike locations are shown on publicly available NOAA navigation charts and Corps hydrosurvey charts. Mariners should use these charts in addition to visual observation when boating around pile dikes in the Columbia River.

Boat Safety Tips

Family & Life - Travel & Outdoors, May 5, 2020

1. Be prepared with a boat safety kit

You can't always predict an emergency, so be prepared for any situation. Your boat safety kit should be kept on board no matter the size of your boat. Below are some essential items your safety kit should include.

- **Flashlight** – A flashlight and extra batteries can help you see around your boat in the dark and allow you to be seen if you run out of fuel or if your craft stalls.
- **Duct tape** – Spring a leak? Temporarily bandage the hole with duct tape.
- **Bucket** – Even if the boat isn't leaking, water may otherwise enter the vessel. A bucket can help you bail it out.
- **First aid kit** – A properly equipped first aid kit, plus the knowledge on how to use it, is vital in case of an accident or medical emergency.
- **Whistle** – As a recognized signal calling for help on the water, a waterproof whistle is another must-have.

- **Ropes** – These are critical for pulling someone in who has fallen overboard, securing your craft to the dock and tying down loose items in extreme weather.
- **Mirror** – A mirror or any reflective object can signal for help.
- **Garbage bags** – Use them as rain ponchos and protection for items on board.
- **Fire extinguisher** – Just because you're on the water doesn't mean you can't have an onboard fire. All passengers should know the location of your fire extinguisher and how to use it.
- **Life jackets** – You should have a U.S. Coast Guard approved life jacket for every person on board. Read on for information on picking out the right life jackets.

2. Bring the proper life jackets

Life jackets do more than simply keep you afloat. Many are designed to turn an unconscious person face up and even help prevent hypothermia. By law, all boats must have a U.S. Coast Guard-approved life jacket for each person on board. Some states also require children to wear life jackets at all times. Choose a life jacket that is right for your height and weight, plus:

- Try it on before purchasing. Fasten the vest, hold your arms straight up over your head and have someone gently pull the top of the arm opening to make sure it fits snugly.
- Auto and manual inflatable life vests can turn an unconscious wearer face up, but they require regular maintenance. They're also not recommended for children under 16 years of age.
- If you're going fishing, look for a life jacket with pockets and straps to easily carry tackle and supplies.

There are many types of life jackets on the market. Make sure the one you buy is appropriate for your on-water activity.

3. Check the weather beforehand

Warm, sunny days are ideal for boating, but you can't always predict when a storm will roll in. Varying gusts of wind and choppy water are signs of an approaching storm. And even if it's a warm spring day, the water could instead reflect winter temperatures. In the event that your boat capsizes or you and your passengers get wet, make sure you have a plan to seek help and get dry.

4. Don't overload the boat with people or equipment

Always follow your boat's capacity restriction. Overloading your boat with passengers or equipment can unbalance your craft.

5. Check for harmful fumes

After refueling your boat, open all the hatches and smell for fumes. If detected, don't start the engine.

Carbon monoxide can accumulate in and around your boat and unexpectedly knock you or your guests unconscious. Be aware of all the places fumes and gases can accumulate, including:

- Inadequately ventilated canvas enclosures
- Enclosed spaces
- Blocked exhaust outlets
- Nearby boats
- When your engine is idling, running at a slow speed or stopped

6. Use common sense on the water

Rules on the water aren't much different than rules on the road. It's important to use common sense, such as staying alert at all times, operating at a safe speed and ensuring that passengers stay safely within the boat's railings.

7. Follow proper anchoring procedures

Having the right anchor isn't enough. To keep the wind from dragging your boat, you may need to drop two anchors in a V-formation at the front of the craft to keep it from drifting. To help prevent the tide from lifting your anchor, you may need to drop it in deeper water – about 20-30 feet or so.

8. Follow proper docking procedures

Depending on the wind, the current and your type of boat, docking can be a challenge. As you approach the dock or shore, make sure your bumpers are out to prevent damage to your craft, reduce your speed and make sure the docking lines are secured. If the wind is blowing towards the shore, bring the boat about two feet from the dock and the wind will gently pull it in. You can then secure it with lines. If the wind is blowing away from the shore, approach the dock at a 20- to 30-degree angle to compensate for the wind. Then secure the bow line.

9. Take a boating safety course

The U.S. Coast Guard estimates that 70% of boating accidents are caused by operator error. Before you leave the dock, make sure you know the rules and your responsibilities. There are several online courses available, including a few free courses. The Boat US Foundation offers a free online boating safety course developed specifically for each individual state. The U.S. Coast Guard offers an additional list of online and hands-on courses for boating safety.

10. Get your boat checked

The U.S. Coast Guard Auxiliary and the United States Power Squadrons offer free Vessel Safety Checks. There is no charge, and there are no consequences if your boat doesn't pass.

No matter how much you prepare to keep yourself, passengers and your boat safe, accidents can happen. Learn more about protecting your prized vessel with boat insurance.

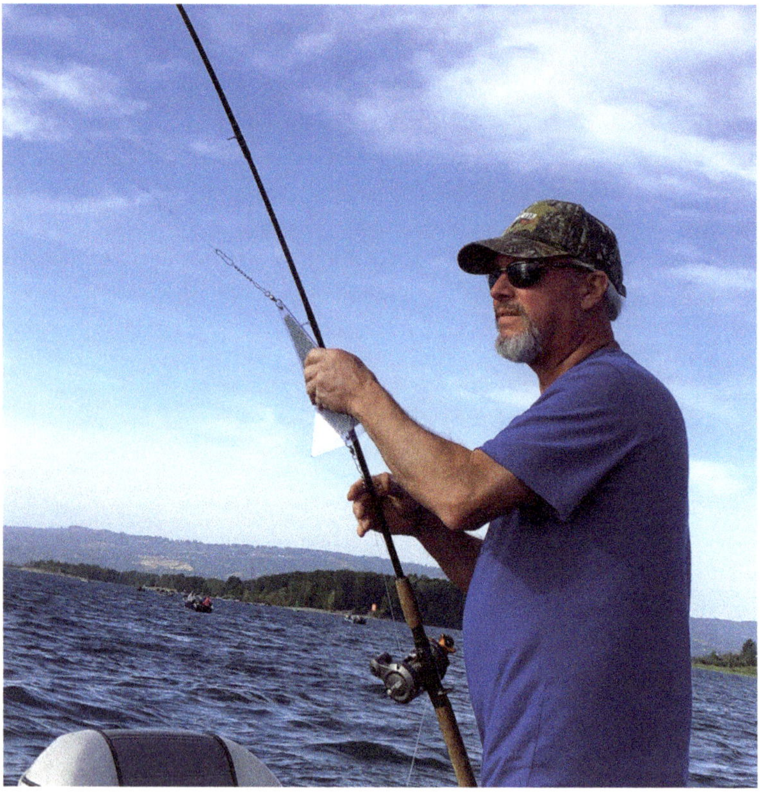

Brother Dan , Expert Fisherman & Story Teller.

Hog Line

Here's what they are on the Columbia River and tributaries: A "**hog line**" is merely a bunch of boats anchored next to each other in a **line** during the salmon runs (spring chinook are often referred to as **hogs**). We anchor in 2-6 mph current, allowing the river to work the lures.

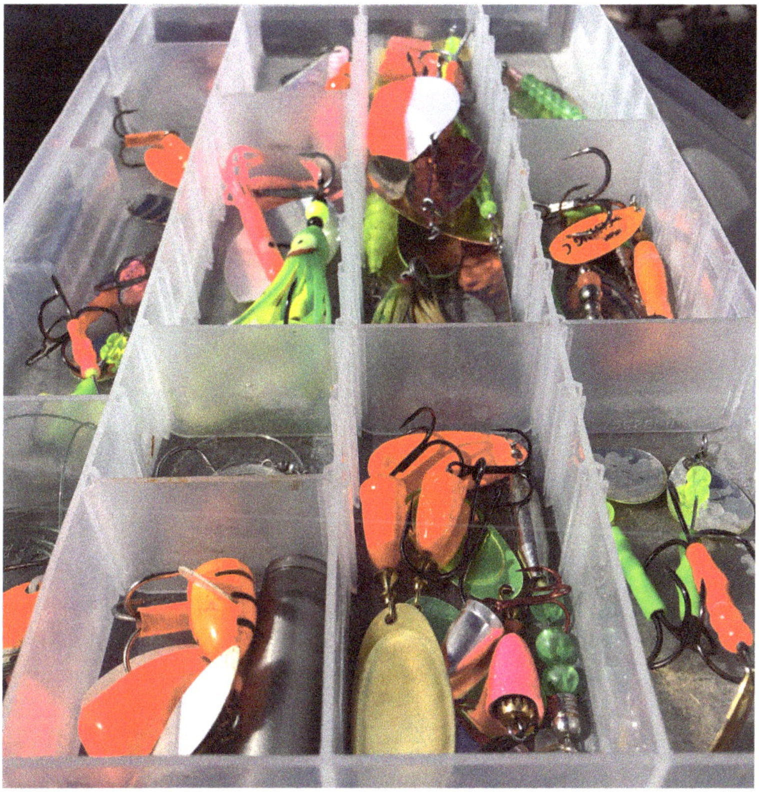

The colorful tackle-box! Rumors advise to wear ones favorite lucky hat.

Get paid to fish

The Northern Pikeminnow Sport-Reward fishery, which pays anglers $5-$8 for each qualifying fish, continues until the end of September.

This program targets large northern pikeminnow, the primary piscine predator of juvenile salmon and steelhead throughout the Columbia and Snake river systems. Tagged pikeminnow are worth $500 each, and in 2019, the top angler earned more than $50,000 – just from fishing!

The goal of the program is not to eradicate pikeminnow, but to harvest 10 to 20 percent of the larger fish that might prey on endangered or threatened salmon and steelhead species.

To see where anglers have been having luck reeling in pikeminnow, visit WDFW's website for weekly updates. For more information on the program and helpful tips on how to catch pikeminnow, visit the program webpage.

Fall Fishing on the Columbia

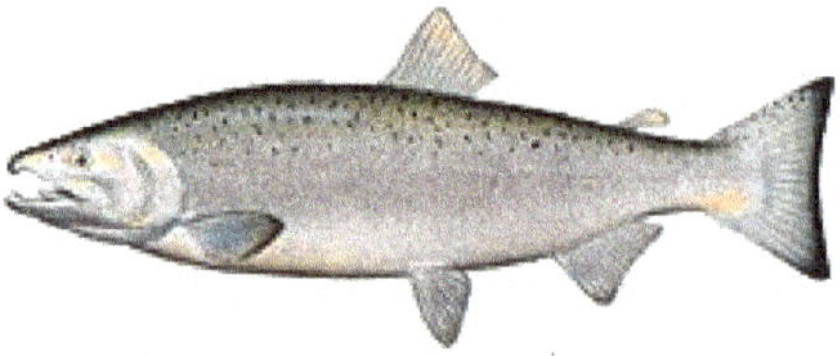

Coho Salmon

During their ocean phase, coho salmon have silver sides and dark-blue backs. During their spawning phase, their jaws and teeth become hooked. After entering fresh water, they develop bright-red sides, bluish-green heads and backs, dark bellies and dark spots on their backs. Sexually maturing fish develop a light-pink or rose shading along the belly, and the males may show a slight arching of the back. Mature adults have a pronounced red skin color with darker backs and average 28 inches (71 cm) and 7 to 11 pounds (3.2 to 5.0 kg), occasionally reaching up to 36 pounds (16 kg). They also develop a large kype (hooked beak) during spawning. Mature females may be darker than males, with both showing a pronounced hook on the nose. wikipedia.com

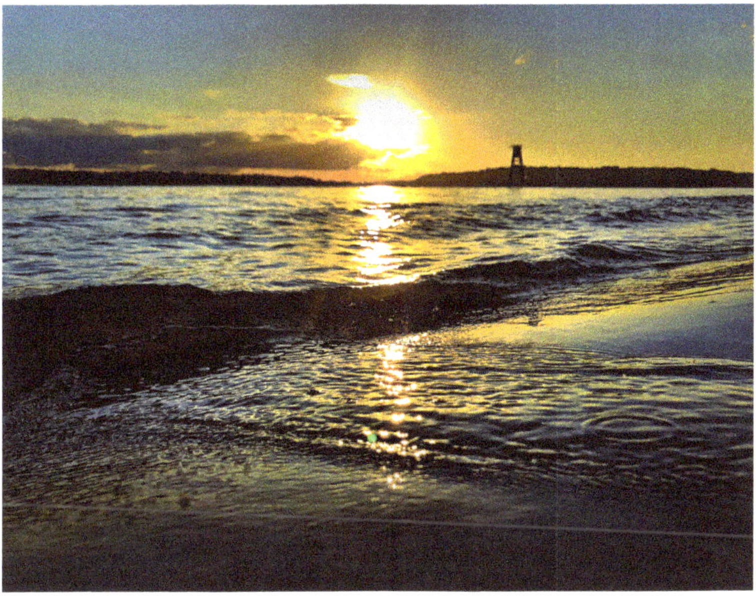

Captain William Clark Regional Park at Cottonwood Beach Washougal Washington

The Great and Beautiful Pacific Northwest is my birthplace and home. As an artist, the massive old growth trees and fish filled rivers have been an undeniable inspiration for my art and music. “If you don't understand how nature heals us. I am here to tell you the truth.” Sometimes life can throw things your way that devastate the life you once knew. Strength is a choice. It's about never giving up. How you respond and react to it defines who you are. Life is like a movie with only one take. Many angles and one shot at this thing. I promised myself at the age of 22. I would not be the old Lady on the front porch in a rocking chair, wishing she had done the dreams and goals she kept to herself. I now am the Lady with a knowing smile on my face. “The one that did!” At the end of it all, we are a paragraph in our local small town Newspaper. What will your paragraph say? Truth........This is also a Love Story. Get outside and feel the magic of nature. Nature can heal your spirit.

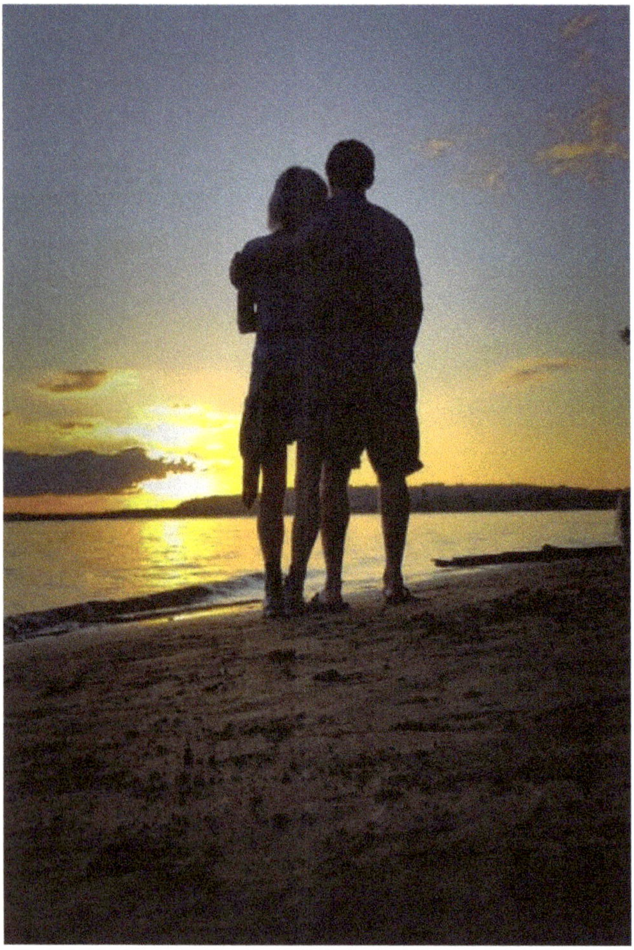

Sunset at Captain William Clark Regional Park at Cottonwood Beach Washougal Washington. “Celebrate Love!” Elizabeth, UpriverStudios

Sources

Ghost Writers & Editors

Wikipedia

Washington Department of Fish and Wildlife

cityofcamas.us

Freelance Writer: Carter Reschke

Freelance Writer: Matt Klems

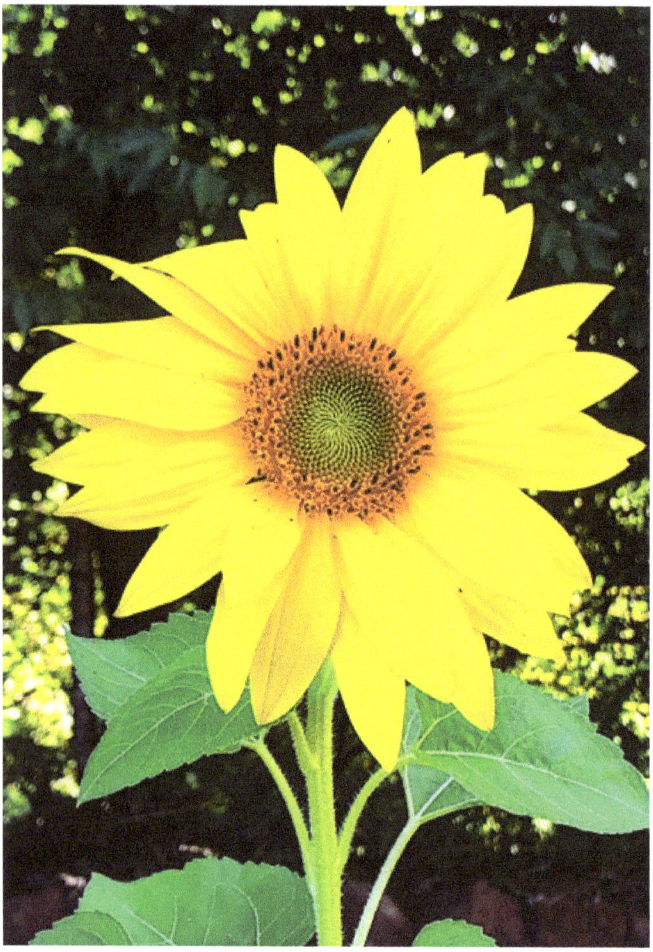

Most grateful with honor and respect to all of you that support my music and other efforts. Hats off!

Oregon Discovery

WTA.ORG (Washington Trails Association)

theoutofbound.com

Seattle Times

parks.state.wa.us

lewistalk.com

gettyphotos.com

youtube.com/recipies

Your Journal

A place for you to write notes, memories or recipes of your own.

CPSIA information can be obtained
at www.ICGtesting.com
Printed in the USA
LVHW020003140121
676450LV00027B/757/J

9 781649 693419